**Director of Publications** Joan M. Irwin
**Assistant Director of Publications** Jeanette K. Moss
**Editor in Chief, Books** Matthew W. Baker
**Permissions Editor** Janet S. Parrack
**Associate Editor** Tori Mello
**Assistant Editor** Sarah Rutigliano
**Acquisitions and Communications Coordinator** Amy T. Roff
**Publications Coordinator** Beth Doughty
**Association Editor** David K. Roberts
**Production Department Manager** Iona Sauscermen
**Art Director** Boni Nash
**Electronic Publishing Supervisor** Wendy A. Mazur
**Electronic Publishing Specialist** Anette Schütz-Ruff
**Electronic Publishing Specialist** Cheryl J. Strum
**Electronic Publishing Assistant** Peggy Mason

**Project Editor** Tori Mello

**Cover Design** Boni Nash

**Library of Congress Cataloging in Publication Data**
Walker, Barbara J., 1946–
    Training the reading team: A guide for supervisors of a volunteer tutoring program / Barbara J. Walker, Ronald Scherry, Lesley Mandel Morrow.
        p.    cm.
    Includes bibliographical references.
    1. Reading (Primary)—United States handbooks, manuals, etc.   2. Reading—Remedial teaching—United States handbooks, manuals, etc.   3. Tutors and tutoring—United States handbooks, manuals, etc.   4. Volunteer workers in education—Training of—United States handbooks, manuals, etc.   5. Teaching teams—United States handbooks, manuals, etc.   I. Scherry, Ronald.   II. Morrow, Lesley Mandel. III. Title.
LB1525.76.W35    1999                                                                    99-34951
372.4—dc21
ISBN 0-87207-249-2

Printed in Canada

# Training
## the
# Reading Team

## A Guide for Supervisors of a Volunteer Tutoring Program

Barbara J. Walker
Oklahoma State University
Stillwater, Oklahoma, USA

Ronald Scherry
Billings Public Schools, District #2
Billings, Montana, USA

Lesley Mandel Morrow
Rutgers University
New Brunswick, New Jersey, USA

International Reading Association
800 Barksdale Road, PO Box 8139
Newark, Delaware 19714-8139, USA
www.reading.org

## APPENDIX B **79**

### Overheads and Handouts for the Training Program

# A P P E N D I X   C

## Assessment Tools for Supervisors

# A P P E N D I X   D

## Resources for Tutors

# PREFACE

Children who do not read well are hampered at the very start of their education, which may affect their personal and professional success for the rest of their lives. The goal of the America Reads Challenge, launched in 1996 by U.S. President Bill Clinton, is to ensure that all children can read independently and well by the end of third grade. To reach this goal, America Reads aims to provide 1 million trained and supervised literacy tutors to lend extra support to young children who need help with reading in the early grades. Families, schools, and community volunteers are the foundation of this effort. The International Reading Association Board of Directors endorsed America Reads in a position statement, stating "the [America Reads] initiative is in harmony with research that shows that early, extra support can significantly reduce the number of children who experience long-term severe reading problems" (International Reading Association, 1996).

*Training the Reading Team: A Guide for Supervisors of a Volunteer Tutoring Program* is intended to accompany two books published by the International Reading Association (IRA) to support the America Reads Challenge: *The Reading Team: A Handbook for Volunteer Tutors K–3* and *Tips for the Reading Team: Strategies for Tutors*. The literacy program described in these books is not intended to be a substitute for in-school reading programs or for instruction provided by qualified reading instructors. Instead, the program is designed for volunteer tutors who work with children who have been identified as needing additional support in the early grades.

*Training the Reading Team* recommends that an effective model for implementing a volunteer program makes use of instructional support teams led by reading specialists. Reading professionals can assume a leadership role in these endeavors to ensure close alignment with the programs and needs of schools and children. The suggested instructional support team includes the reading specialist, other school personnel, volunteers who provide tutorial services, and community leaders such as university personnel, directors of after-school programs, and school administrators.

This publication is a resource for those educators who develop and supervise volunteer literacy programs to support young struggling readers. The book provides information—including models, resources, sample training sessions, assessment tools, and handouts—to help supervisors implement a successful program. Furthermore, *Training the Reading Team* outlines a comprehensive program for training volunteers in either school or community settings.

Section 1 discusses ways to begin the process of planning and implementing a tutoring program. A planning model outline and a sample outline have been provided to assist supervisors articulating the purpose and goals of the program, defining the roles of each team member, determining needs, establishing organization, and deciding how the program will be monitored and evaluated. The sample outline presents information from an actual volunteer tutoring program.

Section 2 provides supervisors with complete training sessions on the topics of understanding the tutor's role, training for effective tutoring, and collecting information to monitor success. Each session is formatted to allow the trainer to easily present information. Handouts, overheads, activities, and discussion points also are provided in this section as well as in reproducible form in Appendixes B and D.

This book also includes a variety of assessment tools to enable the supervisor to monitor the progress of the program. These tools—presented in Section 3—are designed to help supervisors, classroom teachers, and reading specialists evaluate the success of individual children, their tutors, and the volunteer program as a whole. Appendix C also gives evaluation forms and checklists that supervisors can copy and use.

In addition to the assessment tools provided, Appendix A includes resources on program planning and implementation. Many of these resources are samples of announcements, letters, interviews, and forms used by successful programs; all will be invaluable to supervisors beginning the program planning process.

*Training the Reading Team* represents the authors' years of experience working with tutors and children. This book's goal is to assist supervisors in planning, implementing, and successfully administering new volunteer literacy programs, which in turn will help achieve the goal of improving children's literacy skills while developing their confidence and motivation as readers and writers.

# Beginning a Reading Team Volunteer Tutoring Program: Teamwork, Communication, and Training

## Selecting the Team and Equipment

Beginning a volunteer literacy program is a large step for any school or agency because volunteers provide an alternative means of delivering educational services to children. Using effective communication, involving all stakeholders in the earliest planning of the volunteer program, and keeping these individuals informed and involved through all phases of the program will help ensure success. An effective volunteer literacy program is built on teamwork, communication, and training.

Reading is a complex process that must be taught by classroom teachers and reading specialists, but the one-on-one support that a tutor can provide is invaluable. Volunteer tutors, however, need appropriate training and a structured program to follow. They also need a supervisor who is available to monitor progress and discuss concerns throughout the tutoring experience.

School districts and community agencies that use volunteers should strive to plan and administer programs that ensure that children's needs are met and their rights are protected. When using volunteers, individual schools and community agencies should

- develop specific policies regarding their programs,
- identify school or agency administrators who are responsible for the appropriate use of volunteers,

- clarify that teachers, not volunteers, are responsible for reading instruction in their classrooms,
- organize the program to allow for regular communication between teachers and volunteers, and
- provide preservice and inservice training for both teachers and volunteers. Part of the training should focus on the roles of the administrator, the reading specialist, the teacher, and the tutor.

Schools and community agencies should not assume that using volunteer tutors will automatically increase the reading performance of children in the program.

To administer a successful volunteer program, the roles of the volunteer support team must be defined. The team described in this manual includes the administrator, the reading specialist, the teacher, and the volunteer. It is important to emphasize that certain tasks should be performed only by certified staff and not by volunteers.

# Including Parents

Parents or family members who care for a child are that child's first teachers. They are also the child's teachers for the longest period of time. It is vital to make parents partners in children's literacy development. Parents can be included in the volunteer tutoring initiative by serving as volunteers or by doing activities with their children at home to support tutoring efforts. Classroom teachers, reading specialists, and tutors should communicate with parents to let them know their child's progress, and parents should be invited to participate in tutoring sessions to see what they are like. However, tutors should only meet with parents under the supervision of the classroom teacher, reading specialist, or the tutor supervisor. Examples of parent activities that can be suggested by volunteer tutors are provided in Appendix D.

# Funding the Project

You will need to consider finding sources to fund your volunteer tutoring project in order to sustain a viable, ongoing program. A program must be structured and well-organized to be successful, and this costs money. Fortunately, many businesses and civic groups may be interested in supporting a literacy program for children. For example, in an America Reads partnership formed between McKinley Elementary School in Billings, Montana, and a local medical center, the center provided funding, a training site, and training materials; paid training costs; and bought special sets of books for the tutors to use with children. Whether your program is a school or a community agency, the following funding source ideas may be worth considering:

- Use district or agency funds.
- Enlist the support of corporate sponsors.
- Build business partnerships.
- Use federal funding designated for America Reads projects.
- Use federal funds such as grants and Title I dollars.
- Write private grants.
- Establish endowments.
- Host fund-raising events.

# Finding a Site

Within your community, there are many sites that would provide an appropriate environment for tutoring, such as schools, a university campus, churches, libraries, and other public buildings that are safe, easily accessible, and covered by the appropriate insurance to avoid liability issues. After arranging for a site, you will need to orient the volunteers to the specifics of the selected site.

# Recruiting Volunteers

Most people who are responsible, literate, and have a strong commitment to helping children can be tutors with appropriate training. As you recruit volunteers, remember that it is not important that they be trained educators because you will provide appropriate training for them to be successful tutors. It is important, however, to recruit people who value helping children and who have the energy and commitment required to work in a volunteer setting. Volunteers should be willing to learn new skills and able to communicate, follow instructions, and use problem-solving skills to enable them to work effectively as a member of the literacy team. They should be sensitive to diversity in cultural backgrounds, lifestyles, and value systems among the children they serve, and they should be able to follow health, safety, and emergency procedures developed by the schools in which they are working.

A school district can partner with a college or university for access to tutors. Colleges and universities involved in community service are a good source of volunteers. Presidents of many colleges and universities have allocated portions of their new work-study allotments for students to be trained as America Reads tutors.

Tutors also can come from community organizations such as churches, synagogues, or local service organizations; senior citizens and parents at home also are wonderful resources. Volunteers also might be recruited from high school service groups, national community service programs such as AmeriCorps, literacy organizations such as the International Reading Association and/or your state and local reading councils, and retired teachers in the community.

Volunteers also can come from a partner organization. For example, in McKinley Elementary School's 1998 partnership with a medical center, the center provided tutors by training 15 medical center staff members. Appendix A, page 60, offers a sample announcement that can be used to recruit volunteer tutors

# Training Volunteers

Training volunteers is imperative. Working individually with young children takes more effort than simply helping teachers make copies for classes, answering the telephone, or running errands. Tutors will develop a close relationship with the child they tutor. The tutoring activities described in *The Reading Team* emphasize being a literacy mentor by actively listening to children read and offering support when they need it. This manual provides an in-depth training program for literacy tutors based on *The Reading Team*, and includes overheads, handouts, and page references to that book to assist supervisors with the process of training volunteers. Although *The Reading Team* gives suggestions for specific books to use in tutoring sessions, the tutoring program it describes can be implemented with any kind of reading program and with many kinds of books.

# Selecting Books for Tutoring

Selecting books that nurture success is critical to a volunteer tutoring program. Finding "just right" books helps to ensure this success. Reading just right books allows children to demonstrate their literacy strengths because they can read enough words correctly to make sense of text. As a supervisor, one of the most critical roles you will perform is helping a tutor find books that fit the abilities of the child he or she is tutoring. Remember, nothing is more motivating than success, and choosing the right books will boost a child's reading and writing success. Appendix D, page 117, suggests titles of easy books and tells how to determine which books might be more difficult.

# Finding and Obtaining Books

There are many places within your community where tutors can find appropriate books. The public library is a good source of books for young children as are curriculum libraries at universities. If you are working in a public school setting, there will be a variety of books in the classroom as well as in the school library. If unsure of his or her student's abilities, a tutor should be encouraged to ask a teacher or librarian for help in selecting books.

Many discount stores and grocery stores have books at the beginning reading level. The Step Into Reading Series (Random House) can be found in most of these stores. Also, bookstores in your town will have a children's section that features many easy-to-read books. This section often will have a wealth of just right books. Some other sources for books are garage sales and stores that sell used books. The books are usually not very expensive, and buying them offers the opportunity for a student to reread books that are familiar because they do not have to be returned. The tutor can even give the book to the program when it is no longer used in the tutoring sessions.

Finally, you may want to order sets of books to develop reading fluency. There are many publishing companies that specialize in predictable books and easy chapter books. Some of these companies give discounts and others give points for each order that you can use to purchase more books. (See Appendix A, page 59, for a list of publisher addresses.)

# Taking Care of Details

Do not forget the details; they can make or break your program. For your program to succeed, you must use a check-in/check-out procedure, prepare tutor packets, assign tutoring areas, make schedules, and orient your volunteers to the program. To help you with this task, this book includes sample forms for you to consider for use with your program (see Appendix A).

# Planning for Success: A Model for Program Development

## Preparing Your Plan

In developing your volunteer program, you will find it useful to have a planning model to follow. The first planning tasks are defining the purpose of the program and identifying the members of the volunteer support team. At this stage, it is important to note the strengths and interests of all the team members in order to best place them within the program.

Next you must determine what the volunteers will do, how children will be selected and assigned to tutors, and how you will monitor and evaluate your program: What performance do you want to see and how will you assess growth? What methods and techniques will be employed to reach the program's stated goals? How specifically will training be conducted, and what is the plan for implementing the program? The planning model outline offered here can serve as a worksheet for answering these important questions before training and implementation begin.

The planning model outline is intended to help program supervisors answer important questions before beginning the formal program development and implementation process. When using the outline that follows, it may be useful to

- outline your goals in general terms; specifics will develop over time,

- give a short proposed method and technique statement wherever appropriate, and

- address specific concerns pertaining to program organization, management, student selection, and volunteer training.

## Planning Model Outline

I. Define purpose and goals
    A. What is the purpose of this program?
    B. What goals do we hope to achieve?

II. Establish the team
    A. Define roles of key team members and note their strengths. Identify tasks to be performed by each person.
       1. School or agency administrator
       2. Coordinator/reading specialist
       3. Teacher
       4. Volunteer tutor

III. Determine training needs
    A. Who are the volunteer tutors?
    B. What will they do?
    C. What types of training will they need?

IV. Determine program organization
    A. How will the program be managed?
    B. How will tutors be introduced to site policies and procedures?

V. Determine how children will be selected
    A. How will children be selected?
    B. Who will determine who is selected?

VI. Determine how the program will be monitored and evaluated
    A. How will program goals be monitored and evaluated?
    B. How will student progress be monitored and evaluated?
    C. How will volunteer tutors be monitored and evaluated?

## Sample Outline for Supervisors

The sample outline that follows provides an example of how supervisors might use the planning model outline to plan for the development and implementation of a volunteer literacy tutor program. The sample responses are shown in italic.

I. Define purpose and goals
    A. What is the purpose of this program?

        *This program will support the America Reads Challenge by using trained and supervised literacy tutors to provide extra support for young children. The program is not intended to be a substitute for in-school reading programs or for instruction provided by qualified reading instructors. It is designed for tutors who work with children whom teachers have identified as needing additional support in the early grades.*

    B. What goals do we hope to achieve?

        *We hope to achieve the goal of building an effective volunteer literacy program emphasizing teamwork, communication, and training. Volunteer tutors will be trained to support school-age children's reading. Tutoring or reading support will not replace regular reading instruction or any special programs that a child may be in; it will serve as added support.*

II. Establish the team
    A. Define roles of key team members and note their strengths. Identify tasks to be performed by each person.
        1. School or agency administrator

           *The administrator will make decisions concerning personnel and their duties, student assignments and schedules, allocation of resources, the applicability of state and federal laws and regulations, and the policies and procedures of the school district or community agency. The administrator will*

- *assist in scheduling children,*
- *develop building, agency, or district policies regarding the use of volunteers,*
- *ensure the safety and well-being of all children and staff,*
- *consult and collaborate with appropriate district, building, and agency personnel,*
- *assure accessibility to all children based on need,*
- *plan for appropriate preservice and inservice training for all involved personnel, and*
- *inform parents and involve them in all aspects of the volunteer program.*

2. Coordinator/reading specialist

*The coordinator/reading specialist will supervise volunteers, advise teachers, and consult and collaborate with both groups. It is the reading specialist's responsibility to implement the training program and to coordinate with the teacher to ensure that volunteers are effectively performing their role so that children are moving toward the achievement of their individualized goals and learning objectives. Volunteers will serve under the supervision of the reading specialist and the teacher. The coordinator/reading specialist will*

- *provide appropriate training for volunteers and teachers,*
- *act as a coordinator between the volunteer and the teacher in the planning process, which includes assuring that assessment takes place to monitor the students' current levels of functioning and growth toward their individual goals and objectives,*
- *participate as a member of the educational team and work with the teacher in collecting, coordinating, and interpreting information about the student in order to assure that the child is working at a level at which he or she can be successful,*
- *coordinate, consult, and collaborate with the building administrator,*
- *prepare and collaborate with the volunteer and the teacher regarding the specifics of the instruction to take place,*

- *monitor, supervise, and evaluate the volunteer assigned to the child, and*
- *inform and involve parents in all aspects of the volunteer program.*

3. Teacher

   *The teacher will serve in a collaborative role with other members of the volunteer support team to ensure that the needs of all the children involved in the program are being met. The teacher will play a vital part in the volunteer program by recommending books that will coordinate with the classroom curriculum. The teacher will*
   - *collaborate with all members of the volunteer support team,*
   - *aid volunteers in carrying out effective student management strategies,*
   - *provide student discipline if needed,*
   - *participate in the portions of the volunteer training that involve teacher/volunteer coordination and communication,*
   - *coordinate with the reading specialist to monitor, supervise, and evaluate the students' growth toward their individual goals, and*
   - *inform and involve parents in all aspects of the volunteer program.*

4. Volunteer tutor

   *Volunteers tutors will assist teachers in providing services related to the instruction and supervision of children. Delivery of instruction will take place only after training by the reading specialist and under the supervision of certified members of the educational team. A volunteer's responsibilities will vary depending on his or her individual skills and the child's needs. A volunteer could be assigned the following responsibilities:*
   - *carry out instruction as outlined in the volunteer training program,*
   - *assist individual children in performing literacy activities initiated by the teacher,*

- *assist the teacher in observing, recording, and charting instructional information,*
- *assist in the preparation, production, and maintenance of instructional materials, and*
- *collaborate with the reading specialist and the teacher in an ongoing review of each child's progress.*

III. Determine training needs

A. Who are the volunteer tutors?

*Tutors will be volunteers from all walks of life. Our program recognizes that with appropriate training, people who are responsible, literate, and commited to helping children can be tutors. By striving to know and understand our volunteers and their needs, we will better be able to outline the type of support we want them to provide to children.*

B. What will they do?

*We will develop a program made up of various components for volunteers to follow, based on those outlined in The Reading Team. We will create a structured routine with specific activities to help volunteers work effectively with students.*

C. What types of training will they need?

*Tutors will receive approximately 10 hours of training spread over at least 2 sessions within a 2-week period. After tutoring begins, the supervisor will be available to the tutor, if necessary. Tutors will meet with the supervisor at least once a month to discuss the tutoring and continue the learning process. Videotapes of training sessions may be made for those tutors who miss sessions or want to review what they have learned.*

*Supervisors will observe tutors about once every 2 weeks to be sure they are developing a good rapport with the child they tutor and are prepared for tutoring sessions. At least once during the tutoring period, the tutor, the supervisor, and the child's teacher will meet to discuss progress. Periodically tutors will meet with the teachers of the children they are tutoring to discuss progress, ask questions, and gain more insight into the progress of children with whom they are working; teachers may offer suggestions for materials during these meetings.*

*The training sessions will include the following components:*

- *Discussion of general rules, policies, and building procedures.*
- *Discussion of tutors' responsibilities, including being on time, attending sessions, being prepared, and keeping records.*
- *Overview of tutoring materials, including tutoring handbook, notebooks, and children's reading materials.*
- *A review of components of the tutoring session as described in* The Reading Team *(pp. 19–26).*

IV. Determine program organization

A. How will the program be managed?

*We will establish a regular routine that is easy for the volunteers to follow, and we will treat volunteers as valued members of our team. The frequency of tutoring sessions will be decided by the teacher, reading specialist, and volunteer tutor. It also will be determined by how often the tutor can participate. Tutoring will take place at least once a week for at least 30 minutes for each student.*

B. How will tutors be introduced to site policies and procedures?

*Part of the volunteers' training will include an orientation to the site, so tutors will know the policies and procedures that may affect them when working with children in this building.*

*Components of orientation for the volunteer will include the following:*

- *safety and emergency procedures*
- *school/agency schedules and important dates*
- *student management procedures*
- *chain of command*
- *accessing needed materials*
- *location and operation of needed equipment*
- *procedure for notifying appropriate persons in case of illness*
- *policies regarding the confidentiality of student information*

V. Determine how children will be selected

    A. How will children be selected?

*This tutoring program is designed for children who are struggling as they begin to read. It is for children who will become fluent readers with the extra reading and writing support that a volunteer can provide. Tutoring is not intended to provide direct instruction for those students who have severe reading difficulties. These students need guided instruction from the specialist and classroom teacher. To complement this instruction, the volunteer may read with these children, but close coordination among the classroom teacher, specialist, and volunteer is needed.*

    B. Who will determine who is selected?

*Classroom teachers and reading specialists will recommend children for the tutoring program based on their determination of the support each child needs. Parents will be informed of their child's selection and must consent to their child's participation in the program. The reading specialist will administer formal and informal instruments to provide information about each student to be tutored. For example, the specialist might obtain an oral reading sample and a writing sample at the onset of the program. Together the teacher and reading specialist can suggest particular materials to use in tutoring each student.*

VI. Determine how the program will be monitored and evaluated

    A. How will program goals be monitored and evaluated?

*To evaluate program goals, summary information will be collected about the program. Tutors and teachers can be interviewed at the program's conclusion. The number of tutors, what organization they represent (for instance, community, university, religious, or professional group), and how much time they spend in the program also can be summarized. The following information will be collected:*

- *number of children participating*
- *average length of sessions*
- *number of sessions each child was tutored*
- *number of tutors and duration of their involvement*

B. How will student progress be monitored and evaluated?
*At each session, the tutor will record the books the child has read and collect writing samples that will be used to monitor and evaluate student progress.*

*Tutors also will use the assessment tools provided in* The Reading Team *to collect further data about the child's motivation, fluency, and retelling ability. Likewise, the supervisor will collect data to help with student and program evaluation.*

C. How will volunteer tutors be monitored and evaluated?
*Tutors need to sign in and pick up their materials when they arrive. After each session, the supervisor will review the "Look What I Did!" form the child filled out, select new materials, and write suggestions for the tutor. Communication remains open between tutor, teacher, and supervisor.*

# Concluding Thoughts

In this first section, we have tried to provide procedures and examples that will help you design your own tutoring program. Although each site is different, we believe the information provided can form a strong basis for beginning a successful tutoring program.

# S E C T I O N  2

## The Training Program

The training program is divided into three sessions:

## SESSION I: Understanding the Tutor's Role
This session provides a general overview and orientation to tutoring and introduces concepts about children's literacy acquisition.

*Part 1: What does it mean to be a volunteer literacy tutor?*
    A. Caring
    B. Coaching
    C. Committing

*Part 2: What is reading, anyway?*
    A. Predicting, revising, and retelling
    B. Becoming a fluent reader

## SESSION II: Training for Effective Tutoring
This session prepares tutors for understanding and working effectively with children and introduces the elements of a tutoring session as outlined in *The Reading Team*.

*Part 1: Before you begin*
    A. Getting to know the child as an individual
    B. Getting to know the child as a student
    C. Finding the right books

*Part 2: Components of the tutoring session (from* The Reading Team, *pages 19–26)*
    A. Read old favorites
    B. Read together
    C. Write together
    D. Read for enjoyment
    E. Talk about words
    F. Summarize success

## SESSION III: Collecting Information to Monitor Success
Introduces record-keeping strategies that can be undertaken by the volunteer.

*Part 1: Recording children's progress*
    A. Keeping records
    B. Preparing summaries
    C. Looking at motivation
    D. Evaluating fluency
    E. Story retelling and rewriting

# SESSION I: Understanding the Tutor's Role

## Part 1: What does it mean to be a volunteer literacy tutor?

### Caring

Tell the tutors the following:

> "As a volunteer you have made a conscious choice to make a difference in a child's literacy development. This choice was precipitated by certain events in your life. Think for a moment about your personal motivation for working with children."

**Activity 1**

- Say to the tutors:

  > "Turn to a person near you, introduce yourself, and share your reasons for volunteering."

- Then ask each tutor to introduce her partner and give her reason for volunteering. As the tutors respond, write their reasons on the chalkboard, chart tablet, or overhead. If issues arise, discuss them briefly.

- If a tutor gives the reason "to learn more about reading and literacy," indicate that you plan to talk more about how children learn to read.

- Summarize the responses listed on the chart tablet or chalkboard.

- When the activity is completed, say,

  > "If learning to read was a simple process, then all people would read easily and we wouldn't need a million volunteers to help children to learn to read. Learning to read is a complex process, though, and you as a tutor can certainly work to build students' competence and confidence. Your enthusiasm is critical in motivating and guiding children. The positive attitudes that you build as you read alongside children should not be overlooked. This is the caring aspect of literacy.

  > "There are several ways to support children's learning and build positive relationships. One way is to use phrases that build trust. You can do this by saying positive things such as, 'I liked the way you told that story,' or 'That was a good response.'"

- Ask the tutors to team with one or two people, and have the group make a list of phrases the tutors might use to support children's learning and build trust.
- When each group has generated a list, have them share one or two phrases by writing them on the chart tablet or chalkboard.
- When the discussion is finished, say,

> "These are good suggestions. Remember that praise that mentions a specific task is most effective. When reading educators talk about a child's *engagement* in reading, they are referring to the child's involvement in the process of reading and his or her understanding of what is being read. Your enthusiasm and support will improve children's reading engagement."

## Phrases to Support Engagement (see Appendix B, page 80)

(see Appendix B, page 80)

Explain that this overhead will give the tutors more suggestions for their lists of phrases that support engagement and the tutoring relationship.

---

Overhead 1

**Phrases to Support Engagement**
- You have such good ideas.
- Wonderful response.
- You got a lot done today.
- You really understand it now.
- Good answer.
- Excellent response.
- I liked how you corrected that.
- Good thinking.

---

After reviewing and discussing these phrases, say,

> "Comment positively when appropriate. Honesty and sincerity will help you to build a relationship. If you give praise for situations in which it is inappropriate or insincere, your praise will not be meaningful. It is not only what you say, but how you say it. Be aware of your tone of voice and your facial expressions.

"One of your goals is to have the child you are tutoring feel that he or she is successful. The smallest improvement will generate a sense of success. And your recognition of those successes will help build a strong bond between you and the child you tutor.

"Sometimes, however, children are not on the right track. You can support their efforts and redirect their thinking at the same time. You will need to use comments like those that appear on this overhead to encourage children to work out their difficulties."

**Show Overhead 2**

## Comments to Use When Children Make Mistakes (see Appendix B, page 81)

Say to the tutors:

"These statements will help you support learning by indicating that the child can figure out a response independently."

---

**Overhead 2**

**Comments to Use When Children Make Mistakes**
- Try that again.
- That wasn't quite right, but you can try again.
- That was a good answer, but what else could it be?
- You're on the right track; keep trying.
- That's close, but think about....

---

## Coaching

Tell the tutors the following:

"You, as tutors, have a unique teaching role. You are not like a teacher who manages 25 children at once. You will work closely with one child and you will be able to coach thinking and learning."

**Activity 3**

- Say to the tutors:

"Think about a time when you were learning something new. It could be when you learned to ride a bike, learned to use a computer, learned to dance, or learned to play basketball. I'll give you a few minutes to think about that experience.

"Now share with your neighbor what that learning experience was like. Did you have to practice? Did it require knowledge of new words, skills, or concepts? Did someone help you? Did someone show you how?"

- After they have shared in pairs, have the whole group share some of the information about how they learned the new task. Write these thoughts on the chalkboard or chart tablet.

## Coaching (see Appendix B, page 82)

Uncover each phrase on the overhead as you discuss it.

**Show Overhead 3**

> Overhead 3
>
> **Coaching**
> You are a coach.
> Share your experience.
> Listen actively.
> Use "I" statements.
> Encourage explanations.
> You are a coach.

Say the following to the tutors:

"Almost all of you mentioned that someone helped you learn. We learn new things with a little help from our friends. They show us how to do new tasks. They coach us and support us as we learn. As you read with the child you tutor, you will find that you are a powerful model of a literate individual, and you will assume the role of a supportive coach."

Say the following to the tutors:

"You are a coach when you share your own experiences. During the tutoring session, there will be many opportunities to share your own literacy. You can easily provide personal examples of your own reading. You can share books you've read, clippings from newspapers, recipes, greeting cards, letters, and e-mail that you use in your everyday life. This sharing of personal literacy will help the child see you as a literate individual.

"There will be many opportunities to talk informally with the child you tutor. You can talk about the common experiences you have. Maybe both of you have been to the same sports event, have seen the same movie, or like some of the same things. Children often lack the chance to talk about their experiences in a personal and supportive environment, but you can give them that opportunity."

Say the following to the tutors:

"You are a coach when you listen actively. As you listen to children discuss stories, listen closely to their ideas so you can connect examples that will extend their thinking. By listening actively, you can easily connect personal examples related to the many topics that are described in books.

"Also, as you listen to children, they begin to expand their language, comprehension, and thinking. Knowing that someone is listening increases our desire to communicate."

Say the following to the tutors:

"You are a coach when you use 'I' statements. When you discuss stories, use 'I' statements demonstrating how you actually thought about the story. To do this, you can say for example, 'I was just thinking that the cat might be the reason Tommy is stuck on blue rock.' This is called thinking aloud, and it is another powerful way to share your thinking and help children make connections."

Say the following to the tutors:

"You are a coach when you encourage explanations. Sometimes you will want to ask children to explain their thoughts and ideas. You might say, 'I think the author is probably trying to say…. What do you think the author is trying to say?' By considering several views, children are challenged to think more deeply. Encouraging children to explain their thinking helps them learn both the meaning and the words in stories."

## Committing

Tell the tutors the following:

"Committing yourself to being a volunteer tutor is a big step. It involves not only a commitment of time, but also a commitment to a personal interaction with another individual that at times can be emotionally draining, and at other times, emotionally stimulating. What you are really committing yourself to is making a difference in the life of a child.

"No matter what your background or life experience, you have something valuable to offer as a tutor. As literacy mentors, your life experiences will help children make connections between their life and literacy. Hopefully, you will also gain something from the tutoring experience. It is often said that when we teach we are the ones who learn the most."

## Committing (see Appendix B, page 83)

Show
Overhead 4

Uncover each word on the overhead as you discuss it, then give the explanations provided here for each word:

| Overhead 4 |
| --- |
| **Committing** <br> Time <br> Relationship <br> Personal resources <br> Professionalism <br> Collaboration |

Time—You will commit to tutor every week or on a regularly scheduled basis.

Relationship—You will develop an ongoing relationship with at least one child, and you will need to learn about the child you are tutoring.

Personal resources—You will apply your knowledge and energy toward learning something about children and literacy by participating in ongoing training.

Professionalism—You are part of a professional team and you are viewed as a professional. You are a professional within the tutoring session and in the school. You will make the commitment to be prepared, to participate in training, to keep records, and to respect established schedules.

Collaboration—You will work collaboratively with a team—the principal, the teacher, the reading specialist, and the parents.

You are not just a volunteer, you are making a commitment to be a critical part of the reading team that touches a student on a one-on-one basis.

# Part 2: What is reading, anyway?

## Predicting, Revising, and Retelling

(For background information on the concepts presented in this session, tutors can review the "Tutors Motivate Success" section of *The Reading Team*, pages 11–13.)

Tell the tutors the following:

"Reading is a problem-solving process in which readers construct meaning with text. They use not only the text, but what they know to construct their interpretation."

**Activity 4**

## The Edge (see Appendix B, page 84)

• Uncover parts of the overhead as described in the text that follows.

**Show Overhead 5**

> ### Overhead 5
>
> **The Edge**
>
> With pawned gems financing him, our hero bravely withstood all scornful laughter that tried to prevent his plan. "Your eyes deceive," he had said. "An egg, not a table, correctly describes this unexplored planet." Now three sturdy sisters sought proof, traveling sometimes through calm vastness, yet more often over rough peaks and valleys. Days become weeks as many doubters spread fearful rumors about the edge. At last, from nowhere, winged creatures appeared, signifying huge success.
>
> (Adapted from Dooling, D.J., & Lachman, R. (1971). Effects of comprehension on retention of prose. *Journal of Experimental Psychology, 88*, 216–222).

• Use a white sheet of paper to cover all but the title on Overhead 5. Have tutors predict what the story might be as you read the title.
   *The Edge*

- Next, uncover the first sentence of text from the overhead. Have tutors make new predictions. Write predictions on a chart tablet or chalkboard. Make three columns for predictions on the title and first two sections.

    [First section]

    With pawned gems financing him, our hero bravely withstood all scornful laughter that tried to prevent his plan.

- Next, uncover the second section. Have the tutors make new predictions or revise their predictions.

    [Second section]

    "Your eyes deceive," he had said. "An egg, not a table, correctly describes this unexplored planet." Now three sturdy sisters sought proof, traveling sometimes through calm vastness, yet more often over rough peaks and valleys.

- Uncover the remaining part of the passage and have participants finish reading the passage on their own. Then ask them to write a summary on their own paper. Then have the participants discuss their summaries in groups.

    [Remainder of passage]

    Days became weeks as many doubters spread fearful rumors about the edge. As last, from nowhere, winged creatures appeared, signifying huge success.

- When you are finished discussing this activity, say,

    "Reading is a process that involves predicting and revising. In this way, we construct meaning with text. As we read, we predict what will happen by making associations between what we already know and what we are reading. The more you know, the more you can understand about what you are reading. When our understanding does not make sense, we revise our thinking.

    "One way to support children's thinking is to help them use what they already know. (See *The Reading Team*, page 12, "Supporting what children know.") As a mentor you can invite the child you tutor to think about what he or she already knows about the topic of a book.

"As we completed the activity, we wrote a summary of the story. Retelling is another way you can help children understand what they read. Deciding what is important is a critical part of retelling. (See *The Reading Team*, page 12, "Using the retelling strategy.") Think about the number of times you have told someone about a headline you read in the newspaper or information you found in a magazine. Retelling is a key process in constructing meaning."

## Activity 5

## Show Overhead 6 and Distribute Handout 1

## Becoming a Fluent Reader

Tell the volunteer tutors the following:

"Another aspect of independent reading is fluency. Reading fluently means being able to read in phrases with a good sense of rhythm. Fluent reading results when we read selections that are easy to read, in which the meaning is understandable and the words are recognizable. We need opportunities to read familiar books and poems over and over again. As readers revisit good books, they become more fluent."

### A Poem for Fluency (See Appendix B, page 85)

Have participants read the poem on Overhead 6 aloud. Then distribute a copy of Handout 1 and have them practice reading the poem to themselves. Finally, have everyone read the poem aloud together again, and then talk about their fluency.

---

**Overhead 6 and Handout 1**

**A Poem for Fluency**
From "Ride a Purple Pelican" by Jack Prelutsky

Kitty caught a caterpillar,
Kitty caught a snail,
Kitty caught a turtle
by its tiny turtle tail,
Kitty caught a cricket
with a sticky bit of thread,
she tried to catch a bumblebee,
the bee caught her instead.

---

# SESSION II: Training for Effective Tutoring

## *Part 1: Before you begin*

This part of the session is based on the "Tutors Build Teamwork" section of *The Reading Team*, pages 7–10.

## Getting to Know the Child as an Individual

At the first session, the tutor will want to get to know the child he or she is tutoring. You can begin this session by telling the tutors about having a conversation about interests:

"To begin building a strong bond between you and the child you tutor, spend time getting to know the child during the first tutoring session by sharing some of your interests. You can both talk about your families and friends. You can share the things you like to do during your free time. You can also talk about favorite television shows and any hobbies you have.

"Your tutoring experience will be a very gratifying one because you will learn a great deal about relating to children and working with families, schools, teachers, and community personnel. Take the time to learn about the child you are tutoring, including learning about his or her life both in and out of school.

"Here is a simple game that can help both you and the child you tutor learn more about each other."

**Activity 6**

• Ask each tutor to find a partner. Ask each person to think of an object that means a lot to them. Then instruct the partners to have each person take a turn telling the other about the object and why it is important to them.

• Explain to the whole group that they might want to ask the child they tutor to bring in an object to talk about during one of the early sessions. Tutors also can bring an object to the session, perhaps a photograph or something else they value.

• Say to the tutors:

"This activity will open the door to conversation and finding out about each other. This sharing is important because using children's interests increases their positive attitudes toward reading. If you are still unsure about starting the first session, then you can ask some of the questions on Handout 2; you will also find this form on page 10 of *The Reading Team*."

**Distribute Handout 2**

## Gathering Information About the Child You Tutor (see Appendix B, page 86)

Handout 2

**Gathering Information About the Child You Tutor**

1. Do you have any brothers or sisters? What are they like? Are they older than you or younger than you?
2. Tell me about where you live? (apartment, house, etc.)
3. How many people live at your house?
4. Does anyone help you with reading and writing? Who?
5. What do you like to do most when you're not in school?
6. Tell me about your friends.
7. What do you like about school?
8. What don't you like about school?
9. What are some of your favorite things? To do with friends? To do alone?
10. Do you like to read? Why?
11. Do you like to write? Why?
12. What is the very best story you ever read?

## Getting to Know the Child as a Student

Tell the volunteer tutors the following:

"As a tutor you also will want to know about the child at school and to find out about his schoolwork from the teacher. First, you want to know what he is learning about reading and writing and what literacy activities he does well. If you are working in a school setting, you need to be aware of the materials the child is using for reading. You can ask the teacher questions such as:

1. How is the child doing with schoolwork?
2. What type of help is needed?
3. What materials and strategies is the child working with in reading and writing?

"Using the information you have gained from the child and the teacher, you will be better able to support the child's interests and needs."

## Finding the Right Books

Tell the tutors the following:

"Finding books that fit your student's interests and abilities will mean success for both you and the student. In most programs, the reading specialist will help you identify books that are appropriate for the child you are tutoring. You will need to keep close at hand any books you and your child have already read and enjoyed. We refer to these books as 'old favorites.'

"You also will introduce a new book during each session, and selecting this book will become a major part of your planning. By carefully selecting books that are just right for your student, you can ensure his or her success. 'Just right' means not too hard and not too easy. A book is too difficult when the child makes too many mistakes after you have read it once to the child and then you have read it a second time together. One way to find appropriate books is to use the 'Rule of Thumb' that follows (also found on page 17 of *The Reading Team*)."

## Rule of Thumb (see Appendix B, page 87)

| Overhead 7 |
| --- |
| **Rule of Thumb**<br>1. Choose a book.<br>2. Open it anywhere.<br>3. Make a fist.<br>4. Have the student read a page or two (at least 60 to 70 words).<br>5. Put up a finger for each word the child struggles to read.<br>6. If you need your thumb before the end of the passage, the book is too difficult. |

**Show Overhead 7**

## Part 2: Components of the tutoring session (from The Reading Team)

This session is based on "The Six Elements of the Tutoring Session" found in *The Reading Team*, pages 19–26. Each element that follows is explained in detail and related activities are provided. Handout 3 provides a framework and general description of the components of a tutoring session.

**Distribute Handout 3**

**The Six Elements of the Tutoring Session (see Appendix B, pages 88–89)**

Briefly discuss each element and answer any questions the tutors may have.

---

**Handout 3**

**The Six Elements of the Tutoring Session**

**1. Read old favorites—5 minutes**

Tutors should begin each session by reading books we call "old favorites," which are books the child is familiar with and has read before. We recommend rereading at least two old favorites at the beginning of the session.

**2. Read together—5–10 minutes**

In this phase of the session, you and the child you tutor will read a new book. Select something new to read, discuss what might happen by looking at the pictures and thinking about what you already know. As you read the book aloud, stop to discuss what is happening and what might happen next. Invite the child to read with you at familiar places. After you have read the book, have the child read the new selection alone.

**3. Write together—5 minutes**

By writing together, you can demonstrate how you put your ideas in writing. You can both write in your journals, or you can write to each other to create a written dialog.

**4. Read for enjoyment—5 minutes**

Have the child choose his or her own book for silent reading. Choose a book for yourself, too. After your designated time for reading is over, share with each other what you have read.

**5. Talk about words—5 minutes**

Discussing words will help the child to notice characteristics or patterns in words when reading. You can talk about beginning letters, word length, or rhyming words. You will also use the word in a sentence and explain its meaning.

*(continued)*

---

**The Six Elements of the Tutoring Session** (continued)

**6. Summarize success—5 minutes**

Summarizing success helps children talk about what they did well during the tutoring session. Review the session by filling out the "Look What I Did!" form with the child.

---

# Element 1: Read Old Favorites

Tell the tutors the following:

"Tutors should begin each session by reading books we call 'old favorites.' Books are like old friends, and like a visit with an old friend, reading something familiar is fun and supports the reader. We recommend rereading at least two old favorites at the beginning of the session. This should take about 4 to 5 minutes.

"Rereading favorite selections also helps students practice reading and notice features about print and meaning. When words are within the familiar context of a well-known story, they are easy to figure out. Reading old favorites begins the session with a series of successful reading experiences. The following are procedures for reading old favorites (from *The Reading Team*, page 20)."

## Read Old Favorites (see Appendix B, page 90)

**Show Overhead 8**

| Overhead 8 |
| --- |
| **Read Old Favorites**<br>1. Show three familiar books to the child.<br>2. Ask the child to read a favorite one.<br>3. The child reads the story to you.<br>4. Sometimes, the child will forget a word. When this happens:<br>    a. Ask, "What would make sense?"<br>    b. Point to the picture and ask, "What could it be?"<br>    c. Read with him or her to regain the flow.<br>(See *The Reading Team*, page 20, for other suggestions.) |

## Element 2: Read Together

Tell the volunteer tutors the following:

"Everybody loves to learn new things. In this phase of the session, you and the child you tutor will select something new to read, then discuss what might happen by looking at the pictures and asking the child to think about what he or she already knows.

"You can begin by reading the book aloud, and then inviting the child to follow. Continue this supported reading throughout this phase by stopping to discuss what is happening and what might happen next. Finally, the child will read the new selection alone with only minimal support."

## Read Together (see Appendix B, page 93)

**Show Overhead 9**

| Overhead 9 |
| --- |
| **Read Together** |
| 1. Select a story to read. |
| 2. Looking at pictures, discuss with the child what might happen in the story. |
| 3. Read the book aloud; as you read, stop and ask, "What do you think will happen next?" |
| 4. When you finish reading, ask the child to retell his or her favorite part. |
| 5. Read the book with the child and say, "I know you can help me read this." |
| 6. After reading together, read aloud any troublesome phrases. |
| 7. Let the child read the book out loud alone. |
| 8. If the child stumbles, lend assistance to support reading, or ask "what would make sense?" |
| (See *The Reading Team* pages 20–21 for other suggestions.) |

When you are finished discussing the Read Together procedures, ask the tutors to do the following activity:

- Have a selection of books for the tutors to use. Have tutors form pairs and select a book to read together. Ask them to begin the sequence of reading together with one acting as the tutor and one as the child. When they have finished the read-together sequence, have pairs reverse roles.

**Activity 7**

## When is a book too difficult?

When students read aloud on their own, they will often make mistakes, which could mean that the book is too difficult. A book is too difficult when the student is still making five or six mistakes after it is read twice (once by the tutor and once together).

**Troubleshooting**

## What do you do if the book is too difficult?

When a child begins to read and the book is too difficult, he or she will make mistakes even on words they know well. At this time, simply continue reading with the child until the end of the selection, then select an easier book for the next session. Don't put this book in the pile of familiar books that are used for a warm-up. If chosing the right books for your child is challenging for you, consult with the reading specialist or classroom teacher to find easier books.

**Troubleshooting**

# Element 3: Write Together

Tell the tutors the following:

"By writing together, you can demonstrate how you put your ideas in writing. When we write, we have to think about how words are formed and their consistent letter patterns and letter sounds. You can use the activity of writing together to point out letter patterns in words.

"Writing encourages us to think about how words are put together to form meaning. Use one of the following three activities when you are working with a child."

## Write Together (see Appendix B, page 92)

> **Overhead 10**
>
> **Write Together**
> Choose a writing activity for you and your student:
> - **Writing side by side**
>   You each write in your journals about a topic you each choose individually, then share your writing.
> - **I write, you write**
>   By exchanging a journal, together you and your student write a story by taking turns writing sentences.
> - **Written dialogue**
>   Pass a journal back and forth to hold a written conversation.

As you show each activity give the following explanations:

*Writing side by side*—You and the child write your own ideas in your individual journals. After writing for 3–4 minutes, share what you have written.

*I write, you write*—You and the child compose a story together by alternately writing sentences to complete the story.

*Written dialogue*—You and the child write back and forth as if you were having a conversation.

## Support Children's Writing (see Appendix B, page 93)

> **Overhead 11**
>
> **Support Children's Writing**
> Ask the child, "What are you trying to write about?"
> Tell the child to "Write it the way you think it should be."
> Accept the child's attempts at writing.
> Keep encouraging the child to take risks.
> The more a child writes, the more he or she understands about words.
> (See *The Reading Team* pages 21–23 for other suggestions.)

Point to "What are you trying to write about?" and say to the tutors,

"Focus on the meaning in the child's writing by asking 'What are you trying to write about?'"

Point to "Write it the way you think it should be" and say to the tutors,

"When the child is uncertain about how to write, tell him or her to 'Write it the way you think it should be.'"

Point to "Accept the child's attempts at writing" and say to the tutors,

"Accept the child's attempts at writing, even though the spelling may not be accurate. Children need to get their thoughts on paper."

Point to "Keep encouraging the child to take risks" and say to the tutors,

"Keep encouraging your student to take risks and to spell his or her own way. Every time children write, they think about letters, sounds, and words. This encourages children to develop a knowledge of phonics."

Point to "The more a child writes, the more he or she understands about words," and say to the tutors,

"The more children write, the more they notice and look at print and begin to learn what words look and sound like."

Continue the discussion of Write Together by saying to the tutors,

"Nonwriters imitate what writing looks like just as nonreaders pretend to read a book. Often nonwriters write letters they know or the first letter of a word. We call this 'invented spelling' because they are writing letters that seem to fit based on their knowledge of letter-sound patterns.

"As reading together did, writing together provides a powerful model for children. Writing together can take many forms. This next training session will introduce you to a writing activity called Written Dialogue. You also may use one of the other Activities for Writing given on pages 22–23 of *The Reading Team* to support your students' writing."

- Have tutors form pairs and then practice one of the Write Together activities with one person acting as the tutor and one acting as the child.
- Although the stages of spelling development are covered in the assessment section of this book (see pages 51–52), the supervisor may need this information at this point because tutors are curious about invented spelling. You may introduce it at this time, if needed.

### What if a child cannot spell words?

Many young children use invented spelling and sometimes they are hesitant to write in front of someone. If this happens, simply say, "You can write just one letter for a word and read it to me later."

### What if I can't read what the child wrote?

A child may write so many words with invented spellings that it is very difficult for you to figure out what he or she has written. In these instances, have the child read what he or she wrote so you can write it under the message.

## Element 4: Read for Enjoyment

Tell the tutors the following:

"Good readers become good readers by reading. The more they read, the more fluent they become. Although it seems like a simple principle, time is not always set aside in school to read for pleasure. Children need time each day to read silently from materials they select for their own enjoyment. During the tutoring session, you can take time to read for enjoyment, too, and model this behavior to the child. After your designated time for reading is over, share with each other what you have read. Remember that having the child choose his or her own book for silent reading is a critical aspect of this activity."

## Read for Enjoyment (see Appendix B, page 94)

> Overhead 12
>
> **Read for Enjoyment**
> 1. You and your child each find a book to read silently.
> 2. Show each other the books you will be reading.
> 3. Take turns talking about what you think your book is about.
> 4. Read silently for a few minutes.
> 5. Take turns talking about what you have read.
> (See *The Reading Team*, page 23, for other suggestions.)

## Element 5: Talk About Words

Tell the tutors the following:

"Children learn so many words so fast that it is impossible to teach all of them. Instead, children learn new words and new word meanings by reading and writing. Specific words often convey the key ideas and meaning of a passage. If the key word is unfamiliar and a child does not recognize it or understand its meaning, then the passage becomes very difficult to read. You can help children by discussing words so that when they read they will notice features or patterns in words. You also can show children how to use the other words in a sentence to figure out the meaning of an unfamiliar word.

"When you talk about an interesting word each session, you help children use and refine these strategies. In this part of the lesson, you and your child will each select an interesting word from that day's session. You then write this word on the chart titled Words: Bridging the New and the Known (see Appendix B, page 96).

"After you have selected your word, you can each talk about why it is interesting. Then you can each explain its features and what it means. Finally, use the interesting word in a sentence."

**Talk About Words (see Appendix B, page 95)**

> ### Overhead 13
>
> **Talk About Words**
> 1. Each of you select an interesting word.
> 2. Write your words on the chart titled "Words—Bridging the New and the Known."
> 3. Tell why you chose that word.
> 4. Talk about the word's characteristics.
> 5. Each of you explain the meaning of your word and use it in a sentence.

Elaborate procedures by saying the following as you show the overhead:

1. Each of you select an interesting word.

2. Write your words on the chart titled "Words—Bridging the New and the Known."

3. Start by telling the child why you chose your word. Then ask the child to talk about his or her word.

4. Talk about the word and why it is interesting. Notice features or patterns in the word. Think of other words that rhyme with the interesting word. Then ask the child to talk about his or her word in the same way.

5. Explain the meaning of your word and use it in a sentence. Then ask the child to explain the meaning of his or her word and use it in a sentence.

Demonstrate the technique by writing the word *read* on a chalkboard or chart tablet and say, "I chose the word *read* because it seems so simple, yet it is so complex. The word *read* rhymes with *bead, lead, seed, feed, weed*—the *ead* sound can be spelled *ead* or *eed*."

Write the words on the chalkboard or chart tablet.

## Talk About Words Example
### (see Appendix B, page 97)

**Show Overhead 14**

> Overhead 14
>
> **Talk About Words Example**
> My new word *read* rhymes with these words:
>
> | | |
> |------|------|
> | read | seed |
> | bead | feed |
> | lead | weed |
>
> I can use it in a sentence.
>
> I like to read scary stories.

- Have tutors form pairs and then practice the Talk About Words activity with one acting as the tutor and one acting as the child.

**Activity 9**

## Element 6: Summarize Success

Tell the tutors the following:

"Summarizing success helps children talk about what they did well during the tutoring session. Feeling successful is an extremely motivating factor in all life activities, and we tend to repeat activities that make us feel successful. This part of the tutoring plan works to increase motivation and success. By summarizing what went well in a session, you and the student will be motivated to continue those successful activities."

## Distribute Handout 5

### Look What I Did! (from *The Reading Team*, page 26; see Appendix B, page 98)

| Handout 5 |
| --- |

**Look What I Did!**

Name _____

1. Today I read _____ old favorites.

They were _____

_____

_____

2. Today, I read a new book called _____

_____ by _____

What I like about this book is _____

_____

3. Today, I wrote about _____

The part I liked best about writing is _____

4. Today, I chose to read a book for fun called _____

_____ by _____

I chose this book because _____

5. Today, I was good at _____

6. For next time, I will work on _____

_____

## Show Overhead 15

### Summarizing Success (see Appendix B, page 99)

Review each procedure with the tutors.

| Overhead 15 |
| --- |

**Summarizing Success**

1. With the child, discuss the session and fill out the Look What I Did! form after each session.
2. Review the old favorites you read and write the titles of the books on the form.

*(continued)*

**Summarizing Success** *(continued)*

3. Review the new book or passage you read together. Ask the child to think of something he or she likes about the new book and write it on the form.

4. Discuss your writing together. Have the child record what he or she liked best.

5. List the book or book chapter that your child read for enjoyment. Record on the form why that book was chosen.

6. Ask the child to write what he or she did well that day.

7. Ask the child to write what he or she might work on next time.

# Final Review of the Tutoring Session

## The Six Elements of the Tutoring Session

Close this part of the training session by reviewing Handout 3, The Six Elements of the Tutoring Session, a second time with the tutors. Review and discuss each component again and answer tutors' questions. Direct tutors to pages 16–26 of *The Reading Team* for their individual review of the material covered.

**Review Handout 3 again**

# SESSION III: Collecting information to monitor success

## *Part 1: Recording children's progress*

### Keeping Records

Tell the tutors the following:

"This part of the training session explains record-keeping forms and gives examples of children's work to illustrate how student progress can be measured. It is very important to keep records about children's progress in the tutoring program. Records demonstrate the success that the child is experiencing in reading and writing, which will help both the child and you to recognize your success.

"You can help monitor success by keeping a collection of the child's work from each tutoring session. Place items in a manila folder or large envelope. From time to time, you and your student can look over the work he or she has done and discuss progress. These materials may be collected for every tutoring session, or simply at the beginning and end of the sessions.

"*The Reading Team*, pages 27–32, also provides some assessment tools that are fairly simple to administer and understand. These tools will help you keep track of the progress of the child you are tutoring.

"Records that are kept should be shared with the child's teacher, reading specialist, and the individual supervising the tutoring program. Here are some record-keeping strategies:

1. Keep a journal about what you do at each tutoring session.

2. Record the books the child reads.

3. Keep samples of the child's writing from week to week.

4. Record success that the child is enjoying on the Look What I Did! sheet."

## Tutoring Session Record Keeping (see Appendix B, page 100)

Show
Overhead 16

Place a paper over the overhead and uncover each item as you discuss it.

> **Overhead 16**
>
> **Tutoring Session Record Keeping**
> 1. Keep a journal or planning outline.
> 2. Record the books the child reads.
> 3. Keep writing samples.
> 4. Record success on the Look What I Did! sheet.

# Preparing Summaries

Tell the tutors the following:

"One form of measuring progress is summarizing what has been accomplished. At each session, you will have filled out a summary sheet titled Look What I Did!"

Show Overhead 15, Summarizing Success, again. Tell the tutors,

"On this form you recorded how many familiar books were read and the name of the new book that was read. You wrote together, and you recorded information about your writing. You listed the books read for enjoyment and why they were chosen. And you recorded the success the child achieved in the session. This data now can be collected and transferred to a summary sheet to show how much has been accomplished during your tutoring sessions."

## Procedures for Preparing Summary Sheets (see Appendix B, page 101)

Show
Overhead 17

Preview the procedures that will be shown.

> **Overhead 17**
>
> **Procedures for Preparing Summary Sheets**
> 1. Review the activities carried out during the tutoring sessions; for example, reading old favorites , reading a new book, working with words, writing, and reading for enjoyment.
> 2. Summarize the activities on the sheet provided.
> 3. Provide some feedback for the child's parents and your supervisor by summarizing what the child has accomplished.

**Summary of Tutoring (see Appendix B, page 102)**

---

Overhead 18 and Handout 6

**Summary of Tutoring**
Date _____
Child's name _____
Tutor's name _____
Total number of sessions completed _____
Total number of rereadings of old favorites _____
Total number of new books read _____
Total number of books read for enjoyment _____
Total number of words shared _____
The child does well when _____

_____

Comments _____

_____

_____

---

## Looking at Motivation

Provide the following instructions for the tutors:

"It is also important to collect information about student motivation. This can be done easily at the beginning session while you get to know your child and at the final session while you wrap up your tutoring experience. Remember, one of the most important goals that you will accomplish is to help your student increase his or her enjoyment of reading and writing.

"A simple way to collect information about motivation is to use a motivation interview. This will help you to determine the child's feelings about reading and writing by asking questions about their reading habits, their feelings about themselves as readers and writers, and how literacy is encouraged at home."

# Motivation Interview (see Appendix B, page 103)

---

### Handout 7

**Motivation Interview**

Directions: Tell the child that you would like to find out more about what kids like to do and how they feel about reading and writing. Ask each question in the interview and read the multiple choice responses.

How often would you like your teacher to read to the class?
(2) every day          (1) almost every day          (0) not often

Do you like to read books by yourself?
(2) yes          (1) it's OK          (0) no

Which would you most like to have?
(2) a new book          (1) a new game          (0) new clothes

Do you tell your friends about books and stories you read?
(2) a lot          (1) sometimes          (0) never

How do you feel when you read out loud to someone?
(2) good          (1) OK          (0) bad

Do you like to read during your free time?
(2) yes          (1) it's OK          (0) I don't read in my free time

If someone gave you a book for a present, how would you feel?
(2) happy          (1) OK          (0) not very happy, disappointed

Do you take storybooks home from school to read?
(2) almost every day          (1) sometimes          (0) not often

Do you read books out loud to someone in your family?
(2) almost every day          (1) sometimes          (0) not often

What kind of reader are you?
(2) I'm a very good reader          (1) I'm OK          (0) I'm not very good

Learning to read is:
(2) easy          (1) a little hard          (0) really hard

Do you like to write?
(2) yes          (1) it's OK          (0) I'd rather do something else

Do you write in your free time?
(2) a lot          (1) a little          (0) not at all

What do you like to read best?
(2) books and magazines          (1) schoolwork          (0) nothing

---

Adapted from Gambrell, L.B. (1993). Me and my reading scale. In *The impact of Running Start on the reading motivation of and behavior of first-grade children* (Unpublished Research Report). College Park, MD: University of Maryland, National Reading Research Center.

- Distribute the motivation interview and have tutors complete it and then share it with their partner.
- Discuss motivation as a group. Offer the following discussion starter:

"Motivation is critical to reading fluency. When students are motivated to read, they read more frequently on their own, thus increasing their fluency. What are some factors that influence motivation? How can you help increase children's motivation to read and write?"

## Evaluating Fluency

Tell the tutors the following:

"One goal of this program is to help children develop fluent reading. Fluent reading involves reading words smoothly in meaningful phrases. You can evaluate your student's fluency as you listen to him or her read orally. As you listen, ask yourself the following three questions:

Is the child's reading fairly smooth?

Does the child read words in meaningful phrases?

Does the child's voice convey the meaning of the text?

"You can use these questions to rate the fluency of the child's reading. Make a chart with the name of the book, the date, and the fluency rating. By rating the child's fluency when reading both familiar and new books, you can monitor reading progress. Use these ratings during your first sessions with your child and as you are finishing your tutoring experience. This valuable information can then be shared with the reading specialist."

## Fluency Assessment (see Appendix B, page 104)

Overhead 19

**Fluency Assessment**

1. Have the child read a section of the story orally.
2. Listen closely to how the child is reading.
3. Give the oral reading a rating with the following fluency scale.
   - Rating 1 - The child slowly reads one word at a time with many pauses to figure out words and repeats words to figure out meaning.
   - Rating 2 - The child reads slowly with some pauses to figure out words. Occasionally the child reads in phrases of two or three words.
   - Rating 3 - The child reads words in phrases with a lively rhythm and a sense of expression.
4. Record the name of the book, the date, and the fluency rating in your journal or on a chart.

## Show Overhead 20 and Distribute Handout 8

## Summary Chart—Fluency Ratings
## (see Appendix B, page 105)

(see Appendix B, page 105)

Overhead 20 and Handout 8

**Summary Chart—Fluency Ratings**
Child's name _____
Tutor's name _____

| Date | Name of book | New (N) or Familiar (F) | Fluency Rating |
|------|--------------|-------------------------|----------------|
| ____ | _____ | ____ | ____ |
| ____ | _____ | ____ | ____ |
| ____ | _____ | ____ | ____ |
| ____ | _____ | ____ | ____ |
| ____ | _____ | ____ | ____ |
| ____ | _____ | ____ | ____ |
| ____ | _____ | ____ | ____ |
| ____ | _____ | ____ | ____ |
| ____ | _____ | ____ | ____ |
| ____ | _____ | ____ | ____ |
| ____ | _____ | ____ | ____ |
| ____ | _____ | ____ | ____ |
| ____ | _____ | ____ | ____ |

Rating 1 - Reads slowly one word at a time.
Rating 2 - Sometimes reads in two- or three-word phrases, but pauses frequently.
Rating 3 - Reads in phrases with a lively rhythm and a sense of expression.

# Story Retelling and Rewriting

Tell the volunteer tutors the following:

"One goal of tutoring is to increase students' understanding of what they read. Retelling or rewriting a story is one way to do this. In fact, many of our daily interactions involve retelling, so using this as an assessment helps encourage this practice. When you ask a child about a story's setting and the names of the main characters, notice if he or she tells about the main character's problem. Finally, ascertain whether he or she tells the key story actions, includes a resolution to the problem, and then ends the story. Then use the story retelling form to rate the retelling."

## Assessment of Story Retelling and Rewriting (see Appendix B, page 106)

**Show Overhead 21 and Distribute Handout 9**

Overhead 21 and Handout 9

**Assessment of Story Retelling and Rewriting**

Child's name _____ Date _____

Name of story _____

Setting

| | | |
|---|---|---|
| Begins story with an introduction | Yes | No |
| Includes statement about time and place | Yes | No |

Characters

| | | |
|---|---|---|
| Names main characters | Yes | No |
| Names other characters | Yes | No |

Problem

| | | |
|---|---|---|
| Tells about the main character's problem | Yes | No |

Episodes (Story Action)

| | | |
|---|---|---|
| Tells several key story actions | Yes | No |

Resolution

| | | |
|---|---|---|
| Includes the solution to the problem | Yes | No |
| Puts an ending on the story | Yes | No |

Adapted from Morrow, L.M. (1997). *Literacy Development in the Early Years: Helping Children Read and Write* (3rd ed.). Needham Heights, MA: Allyn & Bacon.

## Monitoring Success

Tell the volunteer tutors the following:

> "We've reviewed record-keeping strategies, and we've discussed why it is important to measure children's progress in the tutoring program. Records demonstrate the success that the child is experiencing in reading and writing, and will help both of you recognize where you've been successful and the areas where you may need to improve."

## Concluding the Training Session

You may wish to add additional reviews, discussions, or comments at the conclusion of this training program that are specific to your program or volunteers. It is important to answer any questions the tutors may have, as well as indicate ways they may communicate with you or other members of the team in the future if problems or questions arise. If possible, prepare and distribute a contact list with names and phone numbers of key people involved with the program.

To conclude, say to volunteers,

> "Remember, reading is a liberating force in our lives that allows us to imagine, to challenge and to respond, to think and feel, to make better decisions, and to live life more fully. You will become a reading and writing mentor who offers all these things, along with support and encouragement, to the children you tutor."

# S E C T I O N   3

# Assessment Tools for the Supervisor

The assessment materials presented in Section 2 of this book are easy to understand and administer and can be used by volunteer tutors without much difficulty. There may be a need, however, for additional evaluation measures that allow for closer observation and assessment of children's growth. These additional measures should be administered by the child's classroom teacher, the reading specialist, or the supervisor.

## Assessing Motivation

The supervisor is responsible for the important task of compiling the information obtained by tutors in order to evaluate the effects of the tutoring program. One measure of success would be an increase in children's motivation to read. The supervisor can collect the Motivation Interview forms (see Handout 7 on page 103 of Appendix B) in order to detect an increase or decrease in students' motivation. A form for summarizing and compiling data from motivation interviews is provided in Appendix C on page 108.

## Assessing Oral Reading

One of the most effective ways to assess growth is to conduct an oral reading assessment at the beginning and then again at the end of the tutoring experience. We recommend having the student read a paragraph from an actual text that would be used in the classroom. Selecting 100 words from an actual classroom text allows the supervisor to compare a student's reading with that of other students in the class.

These oral reading records are sophisticated tools for determining a child's reading level and the types of miscues (deviations from the text) he or she makes when reading. The procedures for conducting an oral reading record are as follows:

1. Select a 100-word passage from a book.

2. Have the child read the passage orally

3. Mark each word miscalled on a separate copy of the passage as the child reads aloud. If the child repeats or corrects a mistake, these miscues are not used to compute the score for the passage.

4. After marking the passage, simply divide the number of words miscalled into the total number of words of the passage. This gives you a score for the passage. Also included in Appendix C is a chart titled How to Mark an Oral Reading Record, which gives examples of how to notate the passage to record mistakes and miscues (see page 111).

# Assessing Progress Through Written Retelling

Another recommended assessment involves written retelling. Using the procedure, you can evaluate a child's literacy both at the beginning and at the end of the tutoring experience. Using a story that has just been read, the tutor can simply ask the child to write the story as if he or she was telling it to a friend. You can use this written retelling to evaluate comprehension, spelling development, and writing development. Comparing the beginning and ending scores, you can analyze the child's literacy development.

## Assessing Comprehension

As mentioned in Section II, a written retelling is an excellent way to assess comprehension. You can use the Assessment of Story Retelling and Rewriting form used in the tutor training session (see

Overhead 21 and Handout 9 in Appendix B, page 106) to assess a student's comprehension of a given passage. Instead of using the *yes* and *no* responses on the form, use a ratings scale such as 1 = *represents main ideas poorly*, 2 = *represents main ideas adequately*, and 3 = *represents main ideas exceptionally*. The ratings can then be added together to give a score. If this exercise is done at the beginning of the tutoring experience then periodically throughout, the scores can be compared to assess the child's comprehension achievement.

## Assessing Spelling Development

Children use their own invented spelling, such as using the first letter of a word to represent the entire word or using just the first and last letters of a word. Sometimes, they spell words according to the sounds they hear. Children develop through stages of spelling words. Their spelling often indicates their knowledge of letter-sound relations. Therefore, we recommend analyzing spelling by using a checklist that would reveal a pattern for spelling development in the student's writing. Using the written retelling assessment activity described on page 50, you also can evaluate the student's spelling level.

We have categorized the stages of spelling development as follows: Pre–Sounding-Out Stage, Early Sounding-Out Stage, Sounding-Out Stage, Transitional Spelling, Correct Spelling. (See Stages of Spelling Development, Appendix C, page 110, for a description and examples of these stages.)

Using the written retelling assessment, you may rate where most of the written words fall in the child's writing. For example, one way to interpret the checklist is to say most of the words were represented randomly by letters, which would indicate the pre–sounding-out knowledge stage. Another way to rate the spelling would be to give each category a number: (0) for no words, (1) for a few words, (2) for some of the words, and (3) for many of the words. (See the Spelling Rating Scale that follows. It also is provided in Appendix C, page 109.) This would make the pattern clearer, as children vary in the way they spell individual words.

**Spelling Rating Scale**

Using the rating scale (0 = no words, 1 = a few words, 2 = some of the words, and 3 = many of the words), rate each characteristic:

\_\_\_\_ uses drawing for writing and drawing

\_\_\_\_ differentiates between writing and drawing

\_\_\_\_ uses scribble writing to convey meaning

\_\_\_\_ uses letter-like form

\_\_\_\_ uses and repeats known letters randomly

\_\_\_\_ uses learned letters randomly to convey a message

\_\_\_\_ uses letters that represent some of the sounds in the word

\_\_\_\_ uses most of the letters and some of the sounds in the word

\_\_\_\_ uses sounds as the student hears them (phonetic spelling)

\_\_\_\_ uses a combination of invented spelling and correct spelling

\_\_\_\_ uses correct spelling

## Assessing Writing Development

A checklist for assessing writing development is provided here. (The checklist also is provided in Appendix C, page 112.) As with attempted reading behaviors described earlier, children who are not yet writing will attempt to write. They will draw pictures for writing or do scribble writing that they will use to convey meaning. This checklist can be useful for recording information about children's writing development at the beginning and end of the tutoring program, and can be used to measure progress and success.

**Writing Checklist**

| | Always (3) | Sometimes (2) | Never (1) |
|---|---|---|---|
| Attempts to convey meaning with writing | ___ | ___ | ___ |
| Can write his or her name | ___ | ___ | ___ |
| Asks for words to be written down | ___ | ___ | ___ |
| Copies from books | ___ | ___ | ___ |
| Takes initiative in writng | ___ | ___ | ___ |
| Writes from left to right | ___ | ___ | ___ |
| Leaves spaces between words | ___ | ___ | ___ |
| Uses punctuation correctly | ___ | ___ | ___ |
| Uses capitalization correctly | ___ | ___ | ___ |
| Uses standard spelling | ___ | ___ | ___ |
| Writes complete thoughts | ___ | ___ | ___ |
| Writes three related thoughts | ___ | ___ | ___ |
| Uses descriptive words | ___ | ___ | ___ |
| Views self as a writer | ___ | ___ | ___ |

# Assessing Concepts About Print

This assessment tool allows the supervisor to identify the child's concepts about print, book handling, and reading. The checklist gives an indication of the child's emerging knowledge about how to use printed words when reading. The Print Concepts Evaluation Form is provided in Appendix C, page 113. To administer the assessment, use the following procedures:

> **Print Concepts Evaluation Procedures**
> 1. Hand a book to a child and notice how he handles it.
> 2. Ask the child where to begin reading and where to end.
> 3. Give the child two index cards and ask him to frame a word. Then ask him to frame a sentence.
> 4. Read a sentence of the story and have the child repeat it.
> 5. Ask the child to write a letter in a word.
> 6. Ask the child to write his name and say the letters.
> 7. Fill out the Print Concepts Evaluation Form.
> 7. Analyze what the child understands about how print works. Also, evaluate the knowledge of letter names in the context of a real story. To do this on the Print Concepts Evaluation Form, simply total the number of items in the "yes" column.

# Assessing Tutors

As with all things we do, it is important to reflect on our strengths and weaknesses in any given task. As a supervisor, it is important to be sure that volunteer tutors are reflective about their own tutoring. After each tutoring session, tutors should review the work that was done by the child and determine if the child has made progress. Tutors should think about the relationship they have built with the student to determine if they are building a supportive relationship that enhances the student's self-esteem and supports success. Have tutors keep a log in the back of their writing journal that reflects the events and evaluation of each session. Be sure that each entry is dated.

Meet with tutors on a regular basis. If possible, observe tutoring sessions so you can discuss the tutors' strengths and note areas that you feel need improvement. Perhaps you can videotape a session to encourage self-evaluation. The tutors can talk about their success and concerns related to the children with whom they are working. When you make time for such regular conversations, you can evaluate the progress of tutors as well.

If tutors are working in a school setting, have them discuss the child's progress with the classroom teacher and consult with the teacher frequently to determine if the teacher feels the student is progressing. Have tutors seek input about the materials and strategies used in the regular classroom.

# Evaluating the Tutor's Performance

The Tutor Self-Evaluation Form is designed to help tutors reflect on their work, to assess whether the tutor feels she is helping the child, and to determine if she is enjoying the role of tutor. If the tutor has concerns at any time about her tutoring, you should be consulted. The Tutor Self-Evaluation Form is provided in Appendix C, page 114.

# A Final Word

As a supervisor of a volunteer tutoring program, you are the key to training and coaching the Reading Team. In this book we have provided a program to train volunteer tutors. We also have provided forms and ideas to aid you in assessing the children and the overall program. Although these materials will help you as you begin this endeavor, you must keep in mind that each site is different, and as your program develops, you might need to modify and adapt our suggestions to meet the needs of your community and school.

Your commitment to this project signifies your support of children at risk for learning to read. Volunteer tutors can increase the amount children read and improve their ability to discuss stories with success. The personal support and encouragement of a mentor in a one-to-one setting can increase participation in classroom reading and in reading at home. This increased engagement will contribute to children's reading independence and to their concept of themselves as readers.

Finally, as a supervisor, you will be troubleshooting for and supporting both the children and the volunteers who participate in your program. Your steadfast belief in the power of the mentor-child relationship will sustain the program. You must communicate your commitment to the program while supporting classroom teachers, other specialists, and parents in order to build a team approach to literacy development.

# INTRODUCTION TO APPENDIXES

The four appendixes that follow contain the forms, letters, overheads, and handouts to which the three main sections of this book refer.

Appendix A contains resources for supervisors, including the program planning model outline, a list of sources for obtaining books for the program, sample letters to potential tutors and parents of students chosen for tutoring, and sample interviews and forms for tutors, teachers, and the children being tutored.

Appendix B goes hand-in-hand with Section 2, The Training Program. In this appendix you will find reproducible black line masters of all the overheads and handouts you will need in tutor training sessions. Some of these handouts and overheads are the same, and you will notice both the overhead and handout numbers appear above their titles.

Appendix C provides the supervisor with miscellaneous assessment tools such as forms to help you compile data about student achievement and motivation. There are also checklists and charts to help you monitor and understand student development in reading, writing, and spelling.

Finally, Appendix D gives resources for tutors, including a list of activities that tutors can suggest to parents, how to find "just right" books for children, and a list of International Reading Association publications for tutors. These resource lists can be easily reproduced as handouts for tutors, as well.

# APPENDIX A

## Resources for Supervisors

## Planning Model Outline

I.  Define purpose and goals
    A. What is the purpose of this program?
    B. What goals do we hope to achieve?


II. Establish the team
    A. Define roles of key team members and note their strengths. Identify tasks to be performed by each.
        1. School or agency administrator
        2. Coordinator/reading specialist
        3. Teacher
        4. Volunteer tutor


III. Determine training needs
    A. Who are the volunteer tutors?
    B. What will they do?
    C. What types of training will they need?


IV. Determine program organization
    A. How will the program be managed?
    B. How will tutors be introduced to site policies and procedures?


V.  Determine how children will be selected
    A. How will children be selected?
    B. Who will determine who is selected?


VI. Determine how the program will be monitored and evaluated
    A. How will program goals be monitored and evaluated?
    B. How will student progress be monitored and evaluated?
    C. How will volunteer tutors be monitored and evaluated?

## List of Sources for Obtaining Books

The publishers listed here are recommended because they publish easy reading material, predictable books, and chapter books for young readers. Many are designed specifically to develop fluency.

Dominie Press, Inc.
1949 Kellogg Avenue
Carlsbad, CA 92008
800-232-4570

Harcourt Brace School Publishers
6277 Sea Harbor Drive
Orlando, FL 32887
800-225-5425

Houghton Mifflin Co.
222 Berkely Street
Boston, MA 02116-3764
800-225-3362

Macmillan Publishing USA
Division of Simon & Schuster, Inc.
201 West 103rd Street
Indianapolis, IN 46290
800-545-5914

McGraw-Hill Publishing
1221 Avenue of the Americas
New York, NY 10020
212-512-2000

Modern Curriculum Press
299 Jefferson Road, PO Box 480
Parsippany, NJ 07054-0480
973-739-8000

Rigby Education
500 Coventry Lane, Suite 200
Crystal Lake, IL 60014-7539
800-822-8661

Scholastic Inc.
555 Broadway
New York, NY 10012
800-724-6527

Scott Foresman-Addison Wesley School
     Publishing Group
1900 East Lake Avenue
Glenview, IL 60025
847-729-3000

Seedling Publications, Inc.
4079 Overlook Drive East
Columbus, OH 43214-2931
614-792-0796

Silver Burdett Ginn Publishing
299 Jefferson Road
Parsippany, NJ 07054-0480
973-739-8000

Steck-Vaughn Company
PO Box 26015
Austin, TX 78755
800-531-5015

The Wright Group
19201 120th Avenue NE
Bothell, WA 98011-9512
800-523-2371

## Sample Announcement: Work Experience With Young Children

Become part of the America Reads Challenge. If you decide to join America Reads you will be a reading tutor for children in preschool through elementary school. This year the tutoring will be based in public schools within your local community.

To work individually with young children takes sensitivity and tutors will develop a close relationship with the children they tutor. Because this relationship can have considerable impact on young children, training is imperative. Are you interested in receiving training? If you answered "yes," then tutoring might be for you! Answer the following questions to see if America Reads is for you:

- Do you enjoy children? Do you enjoy seeing the excitement of children as they learn?
- Do you enjoy helping others? Are you relaxed when helping others?
- Do you listen well?
- Do you enjoy reading? Do you easily share your enthusiasm for reading?
- Do you consider yourself responsible?
- Does your schedule allow you to come prepared for all training and weekly tutoring sessions?

## Sample Letter to Potential America Reads Tutors

Date: _____

To:     Interested Tutors
From:   Coordinator, America Reads Tutoring
Re:     America Reads Tutoring

One of the goals of the America Reads Challenge is to give 100,000 college work-study students the opportunity to help children become better readers. Students may be majoring in any discipline, but those in education programs may be most interested in participating. If you decide to join the America Reads team, you will be employed as a reading tutor for children in one of your local elementary schools.

You will work one-on-one with an elementary student following a literacy tutoring program designed specifically for America Reads. This program emphasizes reading, writing, and talking with children as a mentor. We envision you working for 30–40 minutes a session, one session per week, with this student. If your allocation allows, you may tutor two or more different children.

To work individually with young children takes sensitivity, and tutors will develop a close relationship with the child they tutor. Because this relationship can have a considerable impact on young children, training is imperative. The training dates and times will be set once we get a commitment from our volunteers. In this school, you will work closely with your student, the teacher, and other members of the Reading Team.

I will supervise you along with the teacher and principal. You can contact me at [insert contact information here].

Application for America Reads Tutoring Program

Name _____    Major _____

Address_____

Phone_____

1. Have you worked with young children before?    YES    NO
   If yes, describe your experience below:

   _____

   _____


2. The tutoring times can be varied, but they need to fall between 8:30 a.m. and 2:30 p.m., Monday
   to Friday. What times do have available during these times?

   _____

   _____


3. Would you be more interested working between 3:30 p.m. and 6:00 p.m.?    YES    NO

*(continued)*

**Sample Letter to Potential America Reads Tutors** *(continued)*

4. Answer the following questions:

| | | | | |
|---|---|---|---|---|
| Do you read for your own purposes? | A Lot | Sometimes | Occasionally | A Little |
| Do you enjoy young children? | A Lot | Many times | Occasionally | A Little |
| Are you relaxed when you talk with others? | Mostly | Sometimes | Occasionally | A Little |
| Do you like to listen to children? | A Lot | Sometimes | Occasionally | A Little |
| Do you share your own reading? | A Lot | Sometimes | Occasionally | A Little |
| Do you enjoy helping children? | A Lot | Sometimes | Occasionally | A Little |

5. In a paragraph on the back of this sheet, describe why you want to be a volunteer reading tutor.

## Sample Child Pre-Interview

Child's name _____ Grade _____

Teacher _____ Date _____

Gender:    M    F    Birthdate _____

1. Do you enjoy reading? Why or Why not?

2. Are you a good reader? How do you know?

3. Do you read at home? Who do you read with? How do they help you?

4. What do you like to read best? (for example, books, magazines, comics, homework)

5. What do you do when you come to a word you don't know?

6. How do you feel when you read aloud to someone?

7. Who, other than your teacher, helps you with your reading at school? How?

8. Do you like it when someone helps you?

9. Would you like a tutor to help you read at school?

10. What would the tutor help you with?

11. Describe what you think a tutor should be like.

## Sample Tutor Pre-Interview

Tutor's name _____ Date _____

Gender:   M   F   Major _____ Year:   Fresh   Soph   Jr   Sr   Grad

What plans do you have for graduate school and/or a career after graduation?

1. Have you tutored before? If so, what subject? What age group? For how long?

2. Have you ever worked with young children before? If so, how?

3. Why did you decide to be an America Reads tutor?

4. What do you think is the most important thing you can do when tutoring a child?

5. What do you think you will enjoy about tutoring?

6. What do you think will be the most difficult thing about tutoring?

7. What strategies do you think are important in teaching reading?

8. What kinds of materials do you think you could use to tutor students?

9. List the things you would work on if you designed a 30-minute tutoring session.

10. What do you think are the differences in the roles of a tutor and the roles of a teacher?

# Sample Teacher Pre-Interview

Name _____ Date _____

Grade _____ Number of students _____

1. What do think you will like most about using volunteer tutors?

2. What do you think you will like the least?

3. What is the most important thing you would like to see the tutors accomplish?

4. What are the characteristics of the type of child you feel would benefit most from the tutoring process?

5. What suggestions do you have for the project?

6. What strategies do you think the tutors should use to help the children with their reading development?

## Sample Informational Letter to Parents

September 22, 1998

Dear Parents,

McKinley Elementary will soon have community literacy volunteers working as America Reads tutors with our students in grades K–6. The tutors are trained through the America Reads program and will work individually with a child under the direction of the classroom teacher. Your child may be selected to participate in the America Reads tutoring program at McKinley.

Teachers will select students to participate in this program that consists of a one-on-one, 30-minute reading and writing session with the tutor, ____ day(s) a week. This program is designed to strengthen the child's ability to read and write more independently. There will be students of all ability levels involved in the program. The materials used will begin at the child's current level of success and will proceed from that strength.

If you have additional questions, please contact Ron Scherry (Principal) at McKinley. Please sign below only if you do not wish your student to be eligible for participation in the America Reads tutoring program.

Thank You,

- - - - - - - - - - - - - - - - - - - - - - - - - - - - - - - - - - - - - - - - - - - - - - - - - - - - - - - - - - - - - - - - - - - - - -

### Clip, Sign, and Return

I DO NOT wish to have my student participate in the America Reads tutoring program at McKinley this year.

Parent _____

Student _____        Teacher/Grade _____

Date_____

## Sample Letter 1 to Parents of Children Chosen to Participate

October 13, 1998
America Reads
McKinley Elementary

Dear Parent of _____

    Your child has been selected by his/her teacher to participate in the fall 10-week session of America Reads, which will begin next week. He/she will meet with a trained tutor on _____ at _____. During the 30 minutes your child will work on reading and writing skills. Please call if you have questions.

Ron Scherry
Principal

## Sample Letter 2 to Parents of Children Chosen to Participate

September 29, 1998

Dear Parents,

McKinley will begin the America Reads program soon. The program lasts 10 weeks and your child will work with a trained volunteer tutor for 30 minutes, 1 day a week. Students will read and write with their tutor to strengthen their literacy skills.

Your student has been recommended by his/her teacher for the fall session that lasts from October through December. Tutoring times are scheduled during the school day or after school on Tuesday or Wednesday. The after-school sessions meet in the library.

If _____ is available for one of the after-school sessions, please complete the form below and return it to the school.

Grades K–3 stay from 2:30 p.m. to 3:00 p.m. Grades 4–6 stay 3:10 p.m. to 3:40 p.m.

------------------------------------------------------------------------

Clip, Sign, and Return

Yes, (Name) _____ can stay

on Tuesday _____ or Wednesday _____ (Pick one).

He/she is in (Grade) _____ (Teacher) _____

Signed _____     Date _____

He/she will stay to participate in the fall 10-week America Reads program.

## Sample Teacher Input Form—Start of Session

Your Name _____ Grade_____

    Our Fall 1998 volunteer tutoring sessions at [school] will begin in early October. They will run Tuesdays, Wednesdays, and Thursdays for 10 weeks. Please fill out the questionnaire below and place it in the Tutoring folder in [supervisor's] mailbox today. We value your input and need your suggestions in order to develop the program so that it supports your schedule and needs as well as those of your students. Please be sure to include specific reading materials that you would like to see purchased in multiple copies.

| Day | Time | Student's name |
|-----|------|----------------|
| _____ | _____ | _____ |
| _____ | _____ | _____ |
| _____ | _____ | _____ |
| _____ | _____ | _____ |
| _____ | _____ | _____ |
| _____ | _____ | _____ |

Reading Materials
Title _____
Source _____
Cost _____ number of copies _____

Reading Materials
Title _____
Source _____
Cost _____ number of copies _____

## Sample Activity Notice

Dear Teachers:

Please fill out this slip to notify the tutoring program of class activities that will mean students are not available to be tutored. We will pass along the information immediately to tutors. Thank you!

We will be unavailable on _____

In order to: _____

_____

_____

Tutoring time/day canceled        Student

_____     _____

_____     _____

_____     _____

_____     _____

_____     _____

_____     _____

## Sample Volunteer Work Room Sign-In

Volunteer                   Helping                   Day        Time

_____   _____   _____  _____

_____   _____   _____  _____

_____   _____   _____  _____

_____   _____   _____  _____

_____   _____   _____  _____

_____   _____   _____  _____

_____   _____   _____  _____

_____   _____   _____  _____

_____   _____   _____  _____

_____   _____   _____  _____

_____   _____   _____  _____

_____   _____   _____  _____

THANK YOU FOR YOUR HELP!

## Sample Orientation Handout to Volunteers

I. Volunteer Orientation
   A. As a volunteer, you have made a conscious choice to make a difference in a child's growth toward literacy independence. Deciding to participate in a volunteer literacy program is a big step for you as an individual. Your dedication to this project will make a positive difference in a student's life.
   B. In your folder you will find the following general information:
      1. Map of the school with a school calendar
      2. Interest inventory
      3. Developmental spelling page with print D'Nealian alphabet
      4. Sample lesson plan with explanation
      5. Forms for tutor evaluation and comprehension (retelling stories) and a form for recording lesson
      6. General information (this form)
      7. The books needed to present your lesson
      8. Blank tutor evaluation, comprehension, and lesson forms

II. General Problem Solving
   A. If you have a problem with a student, but it's tolerable, finish the tutoring session. When you get ready to leave, put a note in the folder and/or talk briefly to the teacher. If needed, contact the principal.
   B. If the problem is *immediate* (child refuses to participate) warn him that he will be returned to the classroom, and that the teacher and/or principal will be told why. Ask the student what option they choose. Should the problem continue, conclude the session immediately, return the child to the classroom and follow the steps outlined in A.
   C. If your student discusses or you suspect abuse or neglect, talk privately to the child's teacher and/or leave a note in the folder.

III. Absences
   A. If you are going to be absent, please call the school in advance and leave notice at the office.
   B. If your child is absent, the teacher will send the next child on the waiting list. You can use the grade-level packet of student materials that the teacher provides. Be aware that you may need to introduce the tutoring routine to your new child.
   C. Some days, school is closed due to teacher inservice days or field trips. A current tutoring schedule will be posted in [Room 1].
   D. If the fire alarm sounds, exit the building with your student. Do not go back inside.

*(continued)*

**Sample Orientation Handout to Volunteers** *(continued)*

IV. Other Information
    A. It is appropriate to wish your child a Happy Birthday, Merry Christmas, Happy Easter, etc. However, gifts for the children are not allowed.
    B. We urge volunteers not to become involved after school with these children.

V. Thank you for coming and welcome to the America Reads program at McKinley. Please call or talk to Ron Scherry (Principal and trainer) if you have any questions or concerns.

## Sample End-of-Year Questions for Teachers

Your name _____ Grade_____

    Our Fall 1998 volunteer tutoring program at McKinley has concluded. The Spring 1999 10-week program will begin in January. It will run Tuesdays, Wednesdays, and Thursdays for 10 weeks. Please fill out the questionnaire below and place it in June Robbins's mailbox today. We value your input and need your suggestions in order to develop the program so that it supports your needs as well as those of your students. Your thoughtful response will give us information to share with the tutors during their exit interviews (which begin Tuesday of this week). We thank you for your support and positive comments.

1.  When would you prefer to send students for tutoring next session?
    T_____    W_____    Th_____

2.  We plan to run a fall and spring 10-week session with a 4- or 5-week break around Christmas and no tutoring during September and May.
    Will this work for you?    YES _____    NO _____    OTHER? _____

3.  Which students participated this year? _____
    _____
    _____

4.  Did you see growth in the children you sent? _____
    _____
    _____
    _____

5.  What was the most positive thing you observed? _____
    _____
    _____

6.  Please share your comments regarding areas of the program that need improvement.
    _____
    _____

*(continued)*

**Sample End-of-Year Questions for Teachers** *(continued)*

7. The literacy tutoring session currently includes rereading of known books, introduction of/and new reading, and journal writing and vocabulary building. What other literacy skills support would be useful at your grade level? _____

_____

8. What books would you like included? Author _____

Title _____ Publisher _____

Cost _____     Type _____

# Sample Employer Disclosure Affidavit

(Please read carefully)

Our agency screens prospective employees and volunteers to evaluate whether an applicant poses a risk of harm to the children he or she serves. Information obtained is not an automatic bar to employment or volunteer work, but it is considered in view of all relevant circumstances. This disclosure is required to be completed by former employers in order for the applicant to be considered.

Applicant: _____

PLEASE PRINT COMPLETE NAME AND SOCIAL SECURITY NUMBER

As an agent of the former employer of the undersigned applicant, I affirm to the best of my knowledge that the undersigned HAS NOT at ANY TIME:

Yes    No    (Initial if answer is yes or no and provide information for a "yes" answer on the next page)

___    ___    Been convicted of;

___    ___    Pleaded guilty to (whether or not resulting in a conviction);

___    ___    Pleaded no contest to;

___    ___    Admitted;

___    ___    Had any judgment or order rendered against him/her (whether by default or otherwise);

___    ___    Entered into any settlement of an action or claim of;

___    ___    Had any license, certificate, or employment suspended, revoked, terminated, or affected adversely because of;

___    ___    Been diagnosed as having or treated for any mental or emotional condition arising from; or

___    ___    Resigned under threat of termination of employment or volunteer work for.

Any allegation, any conduct, matter of thing (irrespective of the formal name thereof) constituting or involving (whether under criminal or civil law of any jurisdiction):

Yes    No    (Initial if answer is yes or no and provide brief information for a "yes" answer on the next page)

___    ___    Any felony

___    ___    Rape or other sexual assault

___    ___    Drug/alcohol-related offenses

___    ___    Abuse of a minor or child, whether physical or sexual

___    ___    Incest

___    ___    Kidnapping, false imprisonment, or abduction

*(continued)*

## Sample Employer Disclosure Affidavit *(continued)*

___   ___     Sexual harassment
___   ___     Sexual exploitation of a minor
___   ___     Sexual conduct with a minor
___   ___     Annoying/molesting a child
___   ___     Lewdness and/or indecent exposure
___   ___     Lewd and lascivious behavior
___   ___     Obscene literature
___   ___     Assault, battery, or other offense involving a minor
___   ___     Endangerment of a child
___   ___     Any misdemeanor or other offense classification involving a minor or to which a minor was a witness
___   ___     Unfitness as a parent or custodian
___   ___     Removing children from a state or concealing children in violation of a law or court order
___   ___     Restrictions or limitations on contact or visitation with children or minors;
___   ___     Similar or related conduct, matters, or things
___   ___     Been accused of any of the above

EXCEPT THE FOLLOWING:
(IF YOU ANSWERED "YES" TO ANY OF THE ABOVE PLEASE PROVIDE INFORMATION BELOW; IF NONE, WRITE "NONE")

Description                                Dates

_____

_____

_____

_____

_____

_____

The above statements are true and complete to the best of my knowledge.

Date_____      Signature _____

Name _____      Title _____

Company _____      Address _____

City/State/Zip _____      Phone _____

## Sample Authorization to Release Information

REGARDING:

Applicant's name:_____

Applicant's current address: _____

_____

Applicant's Social Security number: _____

Agency contact person: _____

Authorization expiration date: _____

I, the undersigned, authorize and consent to any person, firm, organization, or corporation provided a copy (including photocopy or facsimile copy) of this Authorization to Release Information by the above-stated agency to release and disclose to such agency any and all information or records requested regarding me including, but not necessarily limited to, my employment records, volunteer experience, military records, criminal information records (if any), and background. I have authorized this information to be released, either in writing or via telephone, in connection with my application for employment or to be a volunteer at the agency.

Any person, firm, organization, or corporation providing information or records in accordance with this Authorization is released from any and all claims and liability for compliance. Such information will be held in confidence in accordance with agency guidelines.

This authorization expires on the date stated above.

_____        _____
Signature of Prospective Employee                Date

_____        _____
Witness to Signature                                    Date

# APPENDIX B

## Overheads and Handouts for the Training Program

## Phrases to Support Engagement

- You have such good ideas.

- Wonderful response.

- You got a lot done today.

- You really understand it now.

- Good answer.

- Excellent response.

- I liked how you corrected that.

- Good thinking.

## Overhead 2

# Comments to Use When Children Make Mistakes

- Try that again.

- That wasn't quite right, but you can try again.

- That was a good answer, but what else could it be?

- You're on the right track; keep trying.

- That's close, but think about....

# Coaching

You are a coach.

Share your experience.

Listen actively.

Use "I" statements.

Encourage explanations.

You are a coach.

# Committing

Time

Relationship

Personal resources

Professionalism

Collaboration

# The Edge

With pawned gems financing him, our hero bravely withstood all scornful laughter that tried to prevent his plan. "Your eyes deceive," he had said. "An egg, not a table, correcty describes this unexplored planet." Now three sturdy sisters sought proof, traveling sometimes through calm vastness, yet more often over rough peaks and valleys. Days became weeks as many doubters spread fearful rumors about the edge. At last, from nowhere, winged creatures appeared, signifying huge success.

Adapted from Dooling, D.J. & Lachman, R. (1971). Effects of comprehension on retention of prose. *Journal of Experimental Psychology, 88,* 216–222.

# A Poem for Fluency

From "Ride a Purple Pelican" by Jack Prelutsky

Kitty caught a caterpillar,

Kitty caught a snail,

Kitty caught a turtle

by its tiny turtle tail,

Kitty caught a cricket

with a sticky bit of thread,

she tried to catch a bumblebee,

the bee caught her instead.

---

# Gathering Information About the Child You Tutor

1. Do you have any brothers or sisters? What are they like? Are they older than you or younger than you?
2. Tell me about where you live? (apartment, house, etc.)
3. How many people live at your house?
4. Does anyone help you with reading and writing? Who?
5. What do you like to do most when you're not in school?
6. Tell me about your friends.
7. What do you like about school?
8. What don't you like about school?
9. What are some of your favorite things? To do with friends? To do alone?
10. Do you like to read? Why?
11. Do you like to write? Why?
12. What is the very best story you ever read?

---

# Rule of Thumb

1. Choose a book.

2. Open it anywhere.

3. Make a fist.

4. Have the student read a page or two (at least 60 to 70 words).

5. Put up a finger for each word the child struggles to read.

6. If you need your thumb before the end of the passage, the book is too difficult.

# The Six Elements of the Tutoring Session

### 1. Read old favorites—5 minutes

Tutors should begin each session by reading books we call "old favorites," which are books the child is familiar with and has read before. We recommend rereading at least two old favorites at the beginning of the session.

### 2. Read together—5–10 minutes

In this phase of the session, you and the child you tutor will read a new book. Select something new to read, and discuss what might happen by looking at the pictures and thinking about what you already know. As you read the book aloud, stop to discuss what is happening and what might happen next. Invite the child to read with you at familiar places. After you have read the book, have the child read the new selection alone.

### 3. Write together—5 minutes

By writing together, you can demonstrate how you put your ideas in writing. You can both write in your journals, or you can write to each other to create a written dialog.

## 4. Read for enjoyment—5 minutes

Have the child choose his or her own book for silent reading. Choose a book for yourself, too. After your designated time for reading is over, share with each other what you have read.

## 5. Talk about words—5 minutes

Discussing words will help the child to notice characteristics or patterns in words when reading. You can talk about beginning letters, word length, or rhyming words. You will also use the word in a sentence and explain its meaning.

## 6. Summarize success—5 minutes

Summarizing success helps children talk about what they did well during the tutoring session. Review the session by filling out the "Look What I Did!" form with the child.

Handout 3: The Six Elements of the Tutoring Session. *Training the Reading Team: A Guide for Supervisors of a Volunteer Tutoring Program* by Barbara J. Walker, Ronald Scherry, and Lesley Mandel Morrow. Copyright 1999 by the International Reading Association. May be copied for tutor training only.

# Read Old Favorites

1. Show three familiar books to the child.

2. Ask the child to read a favorite one.

3. The child reads the story to you.

4. Sometimes, the child will forget a word. When this happens:

> a. Ask, "What would make sense?"
>
> b. Point to the picture and ask, "What could it be?"
>
> c. Read with him or her to regain the flow.

(See *The Reading Team*, page 20, for other suggestions.)

---

## Overhead 9

# Read Together

1. Select a story to read.
2. Looking at pictures, discuss with the child what might happen in the story.
3. Read the book aloud; as you read, stop and ask, "What do you think will happen next?"
4. When you finish reading, ask the child to retell his or her favorite part.
5. Read the book with the child and say, "I know you can help me read this."
6. After reading together, read aloud any troublesome phrases.
7. Let the child read the book out loud alone.
8. If the child stumbles, lend assistance to support reading, or ask "What would make sense?"

(See *The Reading Team* pages 20–21 for other suggestions.)

# Write Together

Choose a writing activity for you and your student:

- **Writing side by side**

  You each write in your journals about a topic you each choose individually, then share your writing.

- **I write, you write**

  By exchanging a journal, together you and your student write a story by taking turns writing sentences.

- **Written dialogue**

  Pass a journal back and forth to hold a written conversation.

---

# Overhead 11

## Support Children's Writing

Ask the child, "What are you trying to write about?"

Tell the child to "Write it the way you think it should be."

Accept the child's attempts at writing.

Keep encouraging the child to take risks.

The more a child writes, the more he or she understands about words.

(See *The Reading Team* pages 21–23 for other suggestions.)

# Read for Enjoyment

1. You and your child each find a book to read silently.

2. Show each other the books you will be reading.

3. Take turns talking about what you think your book is about.

3. Read silently for a few minutes.

4. Take turns talking about what you have read.

(See *The Reading Team*, page 23, for other suggestions.)

---

# Overhead 13

## Talk About Words

1. Each of you select an interesting word.
2. Write your words on the chart titled "Words—Bridging the New and the Known."
3. Tell why you chose that word.
4. Talk about the features of the word's characteristics.
5. Each of you explain the meaning of your word and use it in a sentence.

Overhead 13: Talk About Words. *Training the Reading Team: A Guide for Supervisors of a Volunteer Tutoring Program* by Barbara J. Walker, Ronald Scherry, and Lesley Mandel Morrow. Copyright 1999 by the International Reading Association. May be copied for tutor training only.

# Handout 4

# Words—Bridging the New and the Known

It's fun to learn and practice new words and to work with familiar words. Record a new word in each of the stones from the new to the known!

# Talk About Words Example

My new word *read* rhymes with these words:

| | |
|---|---|
| read | seed |
| bead | feed |
| lead | weed |

I can use it in a sentence.

I like to read scary stories.

# Look What I Did!

Name _____

1. Today I read _____ old favorites.

They were _____

_____

_____

2. Today, I read a new book called _____

_____ by _____

What I like about this book is _____

_____

3. Today, I wrote about _____

The part I liked best about writing is _____

4. Today, I chose to read a book for fun called _____

_____ by _____

I chose this book because _____

5. Today, I was good at _____

6. For next time, I will work on _____

_____

_____

# Summarizing Success

1. With the child, discuss the session and fill out the Look What I Did! form after each session.

2. Review the old favorites you read and write the titles of the books on the form.

3. Review the new book or passage you read together. Ask the child to think of something he or she likes about the new book and write it on the form.

4. Discuss your writing together. Have the child record what he or she liked best.

5. List the book or book chapter that your child read for enjoyment. Record on the form why that book was chosen.

6. Ask the child to write what he or she did well that day.

7. Ask the child to write what he or she might work on next time.

# Tutoring Session Record Keeping

1. Keep a journal or planning outline.

2. Record the books the child reads.

3. Keep writing samples.

4. Record success on the Look What I Did! sheet.

Overhead 16: Tutoring Session Record Keeping. *Training the Reading Team: A Guide for Supervisors of a Volunteer Tutoring Program* by Barbara J. Walker, Ronald Scherry, and Lesley Mandel Morrow. Copyright 1999 by the International Reading Association. May be copied for tutor training only.

## Overhead 17

# Procedures for Preparing Summary Sheets

1. Review the activities carried out during the tutoring sessions; for example, reading old favorites, reading a new book, working with words, writing, and reading for enjoyment.

2. Summarize the activities on the sheet provided.

3. Provide some feedback for the child's parents and your supervisor by summarizing what the child has accomplished.

Overhead 17: Procedures for Preparing Summary Sheets. *Training the Reading Team: A Guide for Supervisors of a Volunteer Tutoring Program* by Barbara J. Walker, Ronald Scherry, and Lesley Mandel Morrow. Copyright 1999 by the International Reading Association. May be copied for tutor training only.

# Summary of Tutoring

Date _____

Child's name _____

Tutor's name _____

Total number of sessions completed _____

Total number of rereadings of old favorites _____

Total number of new books read _____

Total number of books read for enjoyment _____

Total number of words shared _____

The child does well when _____

_____

Comments _____

_____

_____

# Handout 7

# Motivation Interview

Directions: Tell the child that you would like to find out more about what kids like to do and how they feel about reading and writing. Ask each question in the interview and read the multiple choice responses.

How often would you like your teacher to read to the class?
(2) every day      (1) almost every day      (0) not often

Do you like to read books by yourself?
(2) yes      (1) it's OK      (0) no

Which would you most like to have?
(2) a new book      (1) a new game      (0) new clothes

Do you tell your friends about books and stories you read?
(2) a lot      (1) sometimes      (0) never

How do you feel when you read out loud to someone?
(2) good      (1) OK      (0) bad

Do you like to read during your free time?
(2) yes      (1) it's OK      (0) I don't read in my free time

If someone gave you a book for a present, how would you feel?
(2) happy      (1) OK      (0) not very happy, disappointed

Do you take storybooks home from school to read?
(2) almost every day      (1) sometimes      (0) not often

Do you read books out loud to someone in your family?
(2) almost every day      (1) sometimes      (0) not often

What kind of reader are you?
(2) I'm a very good reader (1) I'm OK      (0) I'm not very good

Learning to read is:
(2) easy      (1) a little hard      (0) really hard

Do you like to write?
(2) yes      (1) it's OK      (0) I'd rather do something else

Do you write in your free time?
(2) a lot      (1) a little      (0) not at all

What do you like to read best?
(2) books and magazines (1) schoolwork      (0) nothing

---

Adapted from Gambrell, L.B. (1993). Me and my reading scale. In *The impact of Running Start on the reading motivation of and behavior of first-grade children* (Unpublished Research Report). College Park, MD: University of Maryland, National Reading Research Center.

# Fluency Assessment

1. Have the child read a section of the story orally.

2. Listen closely to how the child is reading.

3. Give the oral reading a rating with the following fluency scale:

   - **Rating 1** - The child slowly reads one word at a time with many pauses to figure out words and repeats words to figure out meaning.

   - **Rating 2** - The child reads slowly with some pauses to figure out words. Occasionally the child reads in phrases of two or three words.

   - **Rating 3** - The child reads words in phrases with a lively rhythm and a sense of expression.

4. Record the name of the book, the date, and the fluency rating in your journal or on a chart.

# Summary Chart—
# Fluency Ratings

Child's name_____

Tutor's name _____

| Date | Name of book | New (N) or Familiar (F) | Fluency Rating |
|------|--------------|-------------------------|----------------|
| ____ | _____ | _____ | _____ |
| ____ | _____ | _____ | _____ |
| ____ | _____ | _____ | _____ |
| ____ | _____ | _____ | _____ |
| ____ | _____ | _____ | _____ |
| ____ | _____ | _____ | _____ |
| ____ | _____ | _____ | _____ |
| ____ | _____ | _____ | _____ |
| ____ | _____ | _____ | _____ |
| ____ | _____ | _____ | _____ |
| ____ | _____ | _____ | _____ |
| ____ | _____ | _____ | _____ |
| ____ | _____ | _____ | _____ |
| ____ | _____ | _____ | _____ |

Rating 1 - Reads slowly one word at a time.
Rating 2 - Sometimes reads in two- or three-word phrases, but pauses frequently.
Rating 3 - Reads in phrases with a lively rhythm and a sense of expression.

# Assessment of Story Retelling and Rewriting

Child's name _____ Date _____
Name of story _____

Setting
    Begins story with an introduction     Yes     No
    Includes statement about time and place     Yes     No

Characters
    Names main characters     Yes     No
    Names other characters     Yes     No

Problem
    Tells about the main character's problem     Yes     No

Episodes (Story Action)
    Tells several key story actions     Yes     No

Resolution
    Includes the solution to the problem     Yes     No
    Puts an ending on the story     Yes     No

---

Adapted from Morrow, L.M. (1997). *Literacy Development in the Early Years: Helping Children Read and Write* (3rd ed.). Needham Heights, MA: Allyn & Bacon.

Overhead 21 and Handout 9: Assessment of Story Retelling and Rewriting. *Training the Reading Team: A Guide for Supervisors of a Volunteer Tutoring Program* by Barbara J. Walker, Ronald Scherry, and Lesley Mandel Morrow. Copyright 1999 by the International Reading Association. May be copied for tutor training only.

# APPENDIX C

## Assessment Tools for Supervisors

## Compiled Data From Motivation Interviews

Summary of motivation interviews for the period of _____

| Child's name | Pretest score | Posttest score | Increase/Decrease |
|---|---|---|---|
| _____ | _____ | _____ | _____ |
| _____ | _____ | _____ | _____ |
| _____ | _____ | _____ | _____ |
| _____ | _____ | _____ | _____ |
| _____ | _____ | _____ | _____ |
| _____ | _____ | _____ | _____ |
| _____ | _____ | _____ | _____ |
| _____ | _____ | _____ | _____ |
| _____ | _____ | _____ | _____ |
| _____ | _____ | _____ | _____ |
| _____ | _____ | _____ | _____ |
| _____ | _____ | _____ | _____ |
| _____ | _____ | _____ | _____ |
| _____ | _____ | _____ | _____ |
| _____ | _____ | _____ | _____ |
| _____ | _____ | _____ | _____ |

Totals

NO._____        _____        _____        _____

Mean (Average)            _____        _____        _____

## Spelling Rating Scale

Student's name _____ Date _____
Evaluator _____
Writing (check one)
written retelling _____, journal writing _____, creative writing _____, other (explain)
_____

Using the rating scale (0 = no words, 1 = a few words, 2 = some of the words, and 3 = many of the words), rate each characteristic:

_____ uses drawing for writing and drawing

_____ differentiates between writing and drawing

_____ uses scribble writing to convey meaning

_____ uses letter-like form

_____ uses and repeats known letters randomly

_____ uses learned letters randomly to convey a message

_____ uses letters that represent some of the sounds in the word

_____ uses most of the letters and some of the sounds in the word

_____ uses sounds as the student hears them (phonetic spelling)

_____ uses a combination of invented spelling and correct spelling

_____ uses correct spelling

# Stages of Spelling Development

Pre–Sounding-Out Stage

O                    V

- Letter forms represent a message.
- No sound-symbol relationship.
- Uses letters randomly.

Early Sounding-Out Stage

I                    K

- Whole words are represented by one or more letters.
- The letter(s) represent some of the sounds in the words.

Sounding-Out Stage

IS                   KRM

- Writes a letter for more than half the sounds in a word.
- Usually the letters are hard consonants or long vowels.

Transitional Spelling

ISE                  CREEM

- Knows all words contain vowels.
- Letter-sound relations based on close spelling patterns.

Correct Spelling

ICE                  CREAM

- Conventional spelling using visual memory.

# How to Mark an Oral Reading Record

| Miscue | Definition |
|---|---|

**Substitution**

Text: The girl went to the movie.

Child: The girl wanted to the movie.

Marking: The girl ~~went~~ to the movie. *(wanted written above went)*

A substitution occurs when a child expects a different meaning and substitutes a word that is different from the text.

**Omission**

Text: The girl went to the movie.

Child: The girl to the movie.

Marking: The girl (went) to the movie. *(went circled)*

An omission occurs when the child is thinking ahead and omits a word in the sentence.

**Insertion**

Text: The girl went to the movie.

Child: The girl went to the good movie.

Marking: The girl went to the ʌ movie. *(good written above with insertion caret)*

An insertion occurs when the child adds words to the text.

**Teacher Prompt**

Text: The girl went to the movie.

Child reads: The girl went to the...

Teacher: movie

Child continues: to the movie.

Marking: The girl went to the mᵖovie. *(P marked above movie)*

A teacher prompt occurs when a child hesitates on a word for more than 5 seconds, then the teacher supplies the word.

# Writing Checklist

Date _____

Name _____

Evaluator _____

| | Always (3) | Sometimes (2) | Never (1) |
|---|---|---|---|
| Attempts to convey meaning with writing | ____ | ____ | ____ |
| Can write his or her name | ____ | ____ | ____ |
| Asks for words to be written down | ____ | ____ | ____ |
| Copies from books | ____ | ____ | ____ |
| Takes initiative in writing | ____ | ____ | ____ |
| Writes from left to right | ____ | ____ | ____ |
| Leaves spaces between words | ____ | ____ | ____ |
| Uses punctuation correctly | ____ | ____ | ____ |
| Uses capitalization correctly | ____ | ____ | ____ |
| Uses standard spelling | ____ | ____ | ____ |
| Writes complete thoughts | ____ | ____ | ____ |
| Writes three related thoughts | ____ | ____ | ____ |
| Uses descriptive words | ____ | ____ | ____ |
| Views self as a writer | ____ | ____ | ____ |

# Print Concepts Evaluation Form

Date _____

Name _____

Evaluator _____

**Demonstrates:**

| | | |
|---|---|---|
| how to handle a book | Yes | No |
| where to begin reading | Yes | No |
| how to turn the page | Yes | No |
| how to begin reading on the left-hand page then the right-hand page | Yes | No |
| how to move from the top to the bottom of the page | Yes | No |
| how to begin at the left and go along the line to the right and then return to the next line on the left margin | Yes | No |

**Knows:**

| | | |
|---|---|---|
| concept of words | Yes | No |
| concept of letters | Yes | No |
| words remain the same each time you read them | Yes | No |

**Names:**

| | | |
|---|---|---|
| a letter in a word on the page | Yes | No |
| the letters in unfamiliar words | Yes | No |

# Tutor Self-Evaluation Form

Date _____

Name _____

1. Describe what happened during your tutoring session and list the activities.



2. Describe the behavior of the student. Was he receptive to the tutoring?



3. Describe your rapport with the student. Does the child seem comfortable with you? Do you offer honest, sincere, and positive support?



4. Do you look forward to your tutoring sessions? Why or why not?



5. Do you think the student you are working with is making progress with his reading and writing? Why or why not?



6. Have you received any feedback from the classroom teacher or your supervisor regarding concerns about your work or the student you tutor?



7. Have you received any feedback from the student's parents?



8. Are you pleased that you decided to be a tutor?

# APPENDIX D

## Resources for Tutors

## Activities for Parents: Tips for Volunteer Tutors

It is important to involve parents in connecting volunteer tutoring sessions to home. The following are some suggestions for involving parents:

1. *Read old favorites.* Encourage parents to read something familiar with the child at home. Provide a book that is familiar to the child to take home and read. Simply ask the parent and child to read the familiar book together. Suggest that they discuss the story before it is read and take turns reading. Remind parents that they are valuable resources for retelling family experiences that relate to the story.

2. *Sharing a poem.* At the end of the session, you can read a short poem with the student. Allow the child to take the poem home and read it with his or her parents until the child can read it fluently. Follow these procedures:
   • Have the poem typed on a sheet of paper with space at the top for illustrations.
   • Read the poem aloud to the student and discuss it.
   • Read the poem together.
   • Reread poem until the student can read it alone.
   • Have the child take the poem home and read it with his or her parents and then illustrate it.

3. *Share writing in a journal.* Encourage parents to have a notebook at home to share with their child. You can suggest that they do the shared writing activity together, encouraging the parent and child to talk about what they will be writing about. Also suggest parent and child write individually in their own journals, and read back to each other what they have written. They can write about family experiences, books or stories they have read, or the events of their day. Suggest to parents of children who are not yet writing to accept their child's writing attempts, whether they be pictures, lists of letters, or scribble writing that represents writing.

4. *Reading for enjoyment.* Encourage parents to sit side by side with their child in a comfortable spot when reading together. In addition, parents are encouraged to read to their child books that are too difficult for them to read independently. For children in second grade and third grade, this might mean reading one or two chapters at a time from a chapter book.

# Finding "Just Right" Books for Young Readers
**Tips for Volunteer Tutors**

### Finding "Just Right" Books for Young Readers

Books that help develop children's reading fluency often contain the element of *predictability*. This means the books have language patterns that are repeated throughout, such as, "Little pig, little pig, let me in." If these patterns are repeated on every page, then the book is even easier for children to read independently.

Pictures that show the action and content of the sentences on the page also increase predictability. For example, if the page has a picture of a straw house and the text reads, "The first little pig (a repeated phrase) had a house made of straw," then the sentence is easier to read because the picture provides clues for the words on the page. Thus, young readers can use the pictures to predict what the words say.

Along with predictability, familiar experiences and characters also help develop fluency because the young readers associate what they already know with the words on the page.

To give you an idea of how prediction works, we have provided names of commonly available books that use predictability to foster reading fluency and independence. The books are listed at varying levels of predictability and are used to develop fluency at that grade level.

### First Grade - Beginning of the Year

*Have You Seen My Cat?* by Eric Carle, Scholastic, 1991.
*Have You Seen My Duckling?* by Nancy Tafuri, Morrow, 1991.
*Where Is My Baby?* by Harriet Ziefert and Simms Taaback, HarperCollins, 1997
*Brown Bear, Brown Bear, What Do You See?* by Bill Martin Jr, Holt, 1983.
The topics of these books are familiar and their language patterns are used frequently. Common phrases are repeated on almost every page. The pictures in these books represent the words on the page and thus provide clues for the reader.

### First Grade - Middle of the Year

*Five Little Monkeys Jumping on the Bed*, by Eileen Christelow, Houghton Mifflin, 1989.
*Where's Spot?* by Eric Hill, Putnam, 1980.
*More Spaghetti, I Say*, by Rita Gelman, Scholastic, 1989.
In these books, the topics are quite familiar. The language patterns are less repetitive and include lines that are not repeated in the story. The pictures, however, still provide strong support for figuring out the words.

*(continued)*

## Finding "Just Right" Books for Young Readers *(continued)*

### First Grade - End of the Year
*Goodnight Moon*, by Margaret Wise Brown, HarperCollins, 1977.
*Green Eggs and Ham*, by Dr. Seuss, Random Books, 1960.
*Hop on Pop*, by Dr. Seuss, Random Books, 1963.
*The Napping House*, by Audrey Wood, Harcourt Brace, 1984.
These books maintain the use of familiar topics, but the language pattern is presented as a refrain after each new event. The pictures provide only moderate support for figuring out words.

### Second Grade
*The Very Busy Spider*, by Eric Carle, Putnam, 1985.
*The Very Hungry Caterpillar*, by Eric Carle, Putnam, 1981.
*The Wheels on the Bus*, by Maryann Kovalski, Little, Brown, 1990.
*The Teeny Tiny Woman*, by Barbara Seuling, Puffin, 1978.
*The Three Bears*, by Paul Galdone, Houghton Mifflin, 1985.
*The Cat in the Hat*, by Dr. Seuss, Random Books, 1966.
*I Know a Lady*, by Charlotte Zolotow, Greenwillow, 1984.
These books still have fairly familiar topics, but sometimes the characters' actions are fanciful, such as an old lady who swallows a fly. The language pattern often develops over several pages. The illustrations provide support for overall meaning but not for specific words.

### Finding "Just Right" Books for Slightly Older Readers
As the children begin to read more words fluently, they also need different kinds of books to develop fluency. For readers in the second- and third-grade range, we recommend chapter books because the authors of these books use the same characters and same language structure in each chapter. The chapters provide the predictability that the patterned language did for the younger readers. Interest is also a key in selecting a chapter book, so be sure to allow the child to choose from several books before starting a chapter book. We have listed some easy-to-read chapter books that develop fluency. Remember, the easier, the better.

### Second Grade
Frog and Toad series, by Arnold Lobel, HarperCollins.
Marvin Redpost series, by Louis Sachar, Random House Books for Young Readers.
Pee Wee Scouts series, by Judy Delton, Yearling Books.
Henry and Mudge series, by Cynthia Rylant, Aladdin Paperbacks.

*(continued)*

## Finding "Just Right" Books for Young Readers *(continued)*

**Third Grade**

Amelia Bedelia series, by Peggy Parish, HarperCollins.

Kids on Bus 5 series, by Marcia Leonard, Minstrel Books.

*Hill of Fire*, by Thomas P. Lewis, (HarperCollins) and other "I Can Read" books (HarperCollins)

Magic Tree House books, by Mary Pope Osborne, Random House.

# International Reading Association Tutoring Resources

In the following books, there are many ideas that a tutor can use to vary the tutoring session. At the onset of tutoring, following the recommended procedures is essential. As you get to know the routine and your student, however, you will want ways to spice up your tutoring. These publications can help.

*Beyond Storybooks: Young Children and the Shared Book Experience*
Judith Pollard Slaughter, 1993

This book provides concrete procedures for shared book experiences and collaborative writing and follows the format of the lessons suggested for volunteer tutoring. Many teaching ideas are offered to extend shared reading and writing. An annotated bibliography of more than 100 children's books is included.

*Enriching Our Lives: Poetry Lessons for Adult Literacy Teachers and Tutors*
Francis E. Kazemek and Pat Rigg, 1995

This book provides nine complete, detailed lessons using poetry that will help teachers and tutors. Each lesson focuses on a different type of poetry and is written in a clear, step-by-step format. Poetry is a great medium for developing fluency with second- and third-grade readers.

*So...What's a Tutor to Do?*
Cathy M. Roller, 1998

The concise description of a tutoring session and the principles of good tutoring described in this book will guide even the most inexperienced volunteer tutors.

*Teacher to Teacher: Strategies for the Elementary Classroom*
Mary W. Olson and Susan P. Homan, Editors, 1993

This is a collection of practical ideas from *The Reading Teacher*'s regular column of teaching suggestions. Ideas are grouped into chapters by topic. This is an excellent resource for varying the tutoring session.

*Tips at Your Fingertips: Teaching Strategies for Adult Literacy Tutors*
Ola M. Brown, Editor, 1996

This book contains tutoring tips drawn from articles published in the *Journal of Reading*. Although this book is targeted for tutors of adults, there are many ideas that apply to tutoring all ages.

*The Volunteer Tutor's Toolbox*
Beth Ann Herrmann, Editor, 1994

This book provides general guidelines for getting started tutoring and gives other tips for tutors. It has six chapters that deal with literacy instruction, helping students with classroom work, and assessment. The ideas are practical for anyone tutoring children.

*(continued)*

## International Reading Association Tutoring Resources *(continued)*

These resources focus on specific aspects of the tutoring program, and they can extend your knowledge about literacy and tutoring students to provide support for fluent reading.

*Kids Come in All Languages: Reading Instruction for ESL Students*
Karen Spangenberg-Urbschat and Robert Pritchard, 1994

This book is an excellent resource with many practical suggestions on teaching reading to students who are not native English speakers. Suggestions for using predictable stories and concept books are excellent.

*New Directions in Reading Instruction*
Joy Monahan and Bess Hinson, 1988

This handy flipchart provides valuable information on the way we read and how teaching strategies promote reading. Although targeted for content area reading instruction, there are ideas that fit all ages of readers.

*No Quick Fix: Rethinking Literacy Programs in America's Elementary Schools*
Richard L. Allington and Sean A. Walmsley, Editors, 1995

This book provides suggestions to improve instruction for all children, particularly those who are at risk of not succeeding in today's classrooms. This book embodies the work that formed a basis for our belief that each tutoring session needs to focus on reading multiple books and should coincide with the classroom program.

*Variability Not Disability: Struggling Readers in a Workshop Classroom*
Cathy M. Roller, 1996

This book explains disability as variability, providing a new perspective on why readers struggle. It lays out a practical, day-to-day instructional framework for working with struggling readers in a workshop setting.

## More Resources
These books are invaluable resources for tutoring young children. They are for advanced tutors and their supervisors.

*Reading Recovery: A Guidebook for Teachers in Training*
Marie M. Clay, 1993
Portsmouth, NH: Heinemann.

This book focuses on shared reading and writing used in a volunteer tutoring program. The work of Marie Clay in the field of early reading instruction is a fundamental basis for the design of the familiar and new text parts of the tutoring program. This book also has an excellent section on supporting children when they make mistakes.

*(continued)*

*Literacy Development in the Early Years: Helping Children Read and Write*, 3rd edition
Lesley Mandel Morrow, 1996
Needham Heights, MA: Allyn & Bacon.

This book has many practical ideas for teaching young children and offers theories related to early reading and writing. Many of our assessment suggestions were drawn from this book, which also contains many other suggestions for evaluating early literacy.

*Bridges to Literacy: Learning From Reading Recovery*
Diane DeFord, Carol Lyons, and Gay Su Pinnell, Editors, 1991
Portsmouth, NH: Heinemann.

This volume has many articles that expand on the shared reading and writing used in Reading Recovery. Specific case examples are used to illustrate points. Lists of books that are used in Reading Recovery are found in the chapter on selecting books. Marie Clay also has provided an exceptional chapter on the benefits of this method of instruction.

*Supporting Struggling Readers*
Barbara J. Walker, 2000
Markham, ON: Pippin.

This easy-to-read book focuses on at-risk readers. Its chapter on emergent literacy offers suggestions consistent with the volunteer tutoring program. It also suggests other ways to assess literacy and work with parents.

*Diagnostic Teaching of Reading: Techniques for Instruction and Assessment*, 4th edition
Barbara J. Walker, 2000
Englewood Cliffs, NJ; Merrill/Prentice Hall.

A good resource for supervisors, this book outlines 68 instructional techniques for reading and explains why they work for a particular group of readers.

7213